LET'S BE REAL

LET'S BE REAL

LIVING LIFE AS AN OPEN AND HONEST YOU

BY NATASHA BURE

ZONDERVAN®

ZONDERVAN

Let's Be Real
Copyright © 2017 by Natasha Bure

This title is also available as a Zondervan ebook.

Requests for information should be addressed to:
Zondervan, 3900 *Sparks Dr. SE, Grand Rapids, Michigan 49546*

ISBN 978-0-310-76093-1 (hardcover)

ISBN 978-0-310-76308-6 (softcover)

Cover design: Cindy Davis
Interior design: Denise Froehlich

Printed in the United States of America

18 19 20 21 22 23 24 / LSC / 10 9 8 7 6 5 4 3 2 1

*To my incredible parents, Papa and Mom—
thank you for raising me up in the Lord's
Word and for giving me the most spectacular
life. Without your guidance, never-ending
love, and support, I don't know where I
would be. Thank you for putting up with a
wild child for eighteen-plus years. I love you.*

*To my brothers Lev and Maksim—you
two are my best friends, and I am so
glad I got to grow up with both of you
by my side. Thank you for the laughter,
memories, and stories that I'm going to
keep in my heart forever. I love you.*

CONTENTS

FOREWORD

I first met Natasha when we were both juniors in high school. It was the nineteenth season of *Dancing with the Stars*, and I had been paired up with her mom's previous dancing partner, Mark Ballas. I was thrilled to be introduced to Natasha, because I didn't have a ton of girls my age to hang out with while I was filming in LA. We attended the Movieguide Awards together, and we were dancing like crazy girls in the back of the ballroom while Lecrae performed. Everyone else was sitting and observing the stellar performance, but we didn't care. We sang and danced like no one was watching. We had a blast each and every time we were together, while I was competing and even after I left Los Angeles. Not long ago, we walked in the same Sherri Hill fashion show in New York Fashion Week, which was such a fond memory and a special experience that we got to be a part of together—especially since it was Natasha's first time walking in a runway show. The times that we've spent together have always been filled with laughter and memories that we will have forever.

When Natasha and I first connected, we were both facing issues that pretty much every single teenager faces. She is a super outgoing, passionate, life-loving girl, and she speaks out about these topics in a way you will relate to. *Let's Be Real* really captures the tough stuff teenagers go through, whether it's struggling to be confident or dealing with peer pressure, boy issues, or even staying healthy. Natasha's personal stories and experiences come straight from her life and heart, so it's easy to flip each page and delve into the advice that she gives.

Being a teen isn't easy, especially with society's expectation of what "cool" and "perfection" is—it can often lead us down a rabbit hole. Our lives can be so unpredictable while we are trying to figure out who we are and how we want to live our lives. It can be so easy to listen to the voices that surround us, instead of listening to God's truth and what the Lord has to say about our lives. Learning to be an open and honest you is so crucial to living life to the fullest, and I truly believe that this book can give you the encouragement to do so!

Natasha is here to be real with you—flaws, embarrassing moments, quirks, and all. She's here to talk to you about the issues that some of us don't often want to share with others, because we might not seem "cool." Guess what? That's real life. My message as I speak to everyone is to live original. Who God created you to be. Find the beauty in your heart. So I fully support my girl Natasha teaching readers like you to embrace who God made you to be and figuring out how to navigate life while the world is changing around you—all things *Let's Be Real* is here to help you with.

SADIE ROBERTSON

INTRODUCTION: WHAT'S REAL?

I don't know about you, but I love social media. Not only do I get to engage with thousands of people via Instagram and YouTube, I can express my creativity online. In fact, social media has given me opportunities I never dreamed I would have! And like you, I enjoy looking through other people's posts to find things that inspire me in my life, whether it be with outfits, makeup, fitness motivation, or even some fun recipes to try.

We all know that everything posted online isn't "real." We are all guilty of taking dozens of photos, changing angles and lighting, until it looks *just* right, then tweaking and perfecting until we have the perfect photo to post. Filters on filters just to make sure that it's "Instagram worthy." But to me, the most interesting thing is always the truth hiding behind those images.

What's *my* truth? Well, I'm still figuring life out! And it's going to take some time. But I do know two things: I love God, and music is my passion. Those two focuses have made life much easier for me to navigate, giving me direction and purpose. I have God, who I want to serve and honor, and music, something I can work toward as my career goal!

Let me give you a little background on why truth and being real is so important to me. I've always been a performer—and if you have been to my YouTube channel, that's probably evident!

I started entertaining friends and family when I was little and also sang in church over the years. After high school, I decided not to go to college, instead putting my all into music. I don't recommend that choice for everyone, but I knew what I wanted to do with my life and I knew that this was the time to pursue my dream. Neither of my parents went to college because they both had full-blown careers before they were eighteen. Both have excelled in their very competitive careers—my dad as a former NHL hockey player and Olympian and my mother as a longtime actress and television host. So although they did advise me to go to college first, it wasn't crazy for me to tell them I didn't want to go. I made the riskier choice, knowing that I would have to work as hard as I possibly could and become a mature adult very quickly. Though I'm not in college, I am still working hard to improve my skills, studying dance, singing, and acting—elements I need to focus on for the career I want to pursue. I have to go for it with everything I have. I can't hold back. It's my path. Failure is not an option for me.

As a kid, I was also the most outgoing, bubbly, sassy, center-of-attention little girl you could ever meet. I loved talking to everyone, performing, being competitive, and sharing stories. In elementary and middle school, I was always the one receiving awards for "Most Likely to Become a Star" or "Most Likely to Appear on Broadway." I was constantly putting on shows at home and performing as the lead in school musicals and plays. Later, when I became a bit more tech savvy, I even hosted my own pretend web series called "The Natasha Show."

As a result, my choice to pursue my dream felt like the culmination of a long journey of soul-searching to figure out who I am and what I want my life to look like. I'm still figuring it out, believe me, but I've come a long way; and, as I said earlier, I still don't have it all figured out. But I've learned many things since my early teens, when all I stressed about was what people thought of me and who was posting what on social media.

I joined social media when I was fourteen through Instagram. Immediately, I was bombarded with images of airbrushed models, picture-perfect selfies, and flawless photos of friends and family. Before long, I got caught up in the idea of presenting this facade of perfection as well. I began to post photos that looked more like the images I saw—a made-up, idealized me—than who I really was. I wanted my life to be more like it was "supposed to be"—full of perfect selfies, perfect blowouts, and perfect people.

Social media tends to be about sharing the good times and the times that make us smile. That's because we post what we want other people to see and celebrate online. You rarely see posts about struggles, hardships, mistakes, or failures, because those things can be embarrassing to share. As I began sharing my own experiences, photos, and opinions on social media, I learned how much work goes into the perfect post. And before long I understood how far from reality many things online really are. I couldn't compare myself to what I saw online, because half of those images aren't even achievable in real life. And I couldn't let social media run my life—instead, I had to learn to look at life for what it really is: the raw, cringe-worthy, quirky moments of it all.

The funny thing is, social media is supposed to connect you to other people, but if we only post the flawless moments, we're not actually connecting with anyone because we aren't really being ourselves. When I was agonizing over creating the perfect posts and worrying about what everyone else was doing to look cool, I felt so unsure inside. I was dealing with dark emotions, acne troubles, feeling like I didn't fit in all the time, as well as trying to find out who in the world Natasha was. I grew up in Los Angeles, in a family of five. I am very fortunate to have been brought up the way I was and I'm so thankful. I have the most awesome parents and two annoying but fun little brothers. Yet, at that time, I felt like I didn't have anyone to talk or relate to. They were right there; I could have opened up to any of them, but oftentimes I didn't want to share what was going on inside because I was embarrassed. Even to talk to my friends. Was I going to be judged for the issues I was facing? I wasn't sure if any of them could relate to me, and I really didn't like that feeling.

After I graduated high school at seventeen years old, I reflected on those experiences. There were a lot of moments when I felt alone, isolated in dealing with whatever I was going through at the time. I wish I had been honest and had opened up to my friends and family. It's hard to be vulnerable, I know, but doing so is much more real than pretending to be a perfect version of yourself. In talking to some of my closest friends, I realized we all felt the same way back then—and even now.

> We were all born with flaws that make us who we are.

If I had been brave enough to open up about my issues, maybe my friends and I could have supported each other, commiserated and sought help together. I didn't because I wanted to keep this idea of a problem-free life going—the me I was online. But, of course I had struggles; we all do, just with details changed. And if we can help each other, we should! We were all born with flaws that make us who we are.

It's important to embrace your freckles and your curves. Uniqueness is beautiful. Once we break down the facades and let our true selves out—blemishes, embarrassing moments, mistakes, and all—we welcome others to connect with us on a real level. When I discovered YouTube, I saw it as the perfect outlet to continue the open conversations I once loved as a kid. I embraced my chatty, performance-oriented self. I was able to open up a little more to my viewers and be myself in a way I never had before online—letting out the sometimes silly, sometimes sassy, but always true Natasha. I even keep in the clips of my mess-ups and flubs because they area part of me. I don't film a YouTube video and get it all in one take! Just like with life, no one always gets it right on the first, second, or maybe even tenth try. You have to work at it, and the mess-ups and problems can actually help you grow. Mine show people I'm human, and deep down I know it's good for young viewers, especially, to see that it's not about being perfect. It's okay to mess up.

That's why I'm writing this book. I want to go behind the scenes of everyday life and show our shared struggles and concerns in a real way. I want to help young women be open to embracing their flaws and fears, to be open-minded in accepting and supporting their friends in whatever they're dealing with, and to truly connect with each other. I will share my experiences—the good, the bad, the ugly, and everything in between—so you know you're not alone. We've all been there, dealing with breakouts and breakups, trying to stay true to our faith when social pressures make it challenging, and navigating our teenage years on the road to becoming who we'll be.

I'm not saying I have any magical solutions for dealing with these issues—believe me, if I could cure breakouts and heartbreaks, I would! This book is filled with my tried-and-true tips and advice. And I even brought in friends and family for their input so we can all learn a little something. Life is unpredictable, and complicated, and amazing. It is so much better when we are our true, authentic selves—once we, as young women, support each other through the good and the bad. Once we learn to be real.

—————

I hope the advice and stories you find here will help you feel supported, understood, and confident that the you within is worth setting free.

CHAPTER 1

FIND THE REAL YOU

Be patient.
God isn't finished with you yet.
PHILIPPIANS 1:6 (PARAPHRASE)

I have never been shy. Not a day in my life. When I came out of the womb, I emerged bright-eyed, and once I learned to talk was ready to share my thoughts and opinions. I loved to be the center of attention as a little girl, and from a very young age knew that I wanted to be a star one day. As a six-year-old girl, I didn't know exactly what kind of star I wanted to be. Did I want to be a star athlete? Or a star artist and performer? A star actress? I couldn't quite figure it out, but I did know I wanted to be the best at whatever I pursued.

I remember going into my parents' office when I was about six or seven years old and getting on the computer's PhotoBooth application to record myself. Most kids probably made silly faces or played around with the filters. Not me. Instead, I filmed myself pretending I was accepting an award—a Grammy, a Wimbledon title, a Golden Globe. I had to practice for when I was older, right? But it didn't stop there. If I was walking around the park by myself, if I was in my room alone, if it was only me in the swimming pool, it always seemed like a good time to practice my acceptance speech. I had to get cracking for when they called my name, no matter how far into the future that would be.

Looking back on all those things, I cringe a bit, but I laugh a lot about it too. Little Natasha never cared about what anyone else thought, and that inspires me. She just did what she felt in her heart and she loved it. If you ever want to catch her in action, go to my Instagram account. There are plenty of videos of little me. Although those videos and semi-embarrassing moments make me laugh, they remind me to think like she did. She believed in herself. She never had doubts about her accomplishments. She knew she was going to do great things!

When I was fifteen years old, I started to get into writing music, performing, and singing. These creative mediums became important outlets for me to express myself. At that time my mom told me about the Katy Perry documentary *Part of Me*, which followed her on tour. I vividly remember watching Katy prepare to go out on stage and then walk into the spotlight. I thought to myself, *That's exactly what I want to do*. I knew then that I wanted my own sold-out tours and to sing for thousands upon thousands of people. It just all clicked. I felt it in my gut.

GET TO KNOW YOURSELF

This is an important time in your life—and figuring out what your talents and gifts are, what gets you motivated and excited, and knowing what your boundaries and limits are isn't easy. It's an ongoing process, a part of your life's journey, and you're beginning to experience some of the most important moments in that journey now. It may be through the rules your parents set for you, the pressures you feel from friends and family, or situations that challenge you to question what you believe. And finding out who you are takes wrestling with confusing emotions, teachable moments, extraordinary discoveries, tough situations, and lots of time. There are no quick answers. And I don't know that anyone is ever 100 percent comfortable with who they are—because God is always working on us. But the more we unravel parts of ourselves, the more we begin to live the life that was uniquely made for us.

BREAK THE RULES OR FOLLOW THEM

Honestly, I've never really questioned my parents' values and rules. They taught me so much about morals and faith. They read me the Bible and took me to church every week—they shared the love of Christ with me. Car rides were always filled with conversations about our beliefs and ways to practice our faith every single day. My parents continually taught me to respect others, not lie, not do drugs, never make excuses, stay true to who I am, honor God in all that I do, always work my hardest, and—when in doubt—remember the Ten Commandments. And, my parents had a highly motivating way to help us memorize those commandments; they gave us

> The more we unravel parts of ourselves, the more we begin to live the life that was uniquely made for us.

a dollar each time we recited them. My mom and dad always made time to talk as a family. They have always been strict, but for good reason. They put rules and boundaries in place because they love me and my brothers. Like any teenager, I would get mad at them if I wasn't allowed to do something, but I knew, deep down, it was in my best interest.

How I grew up and matured had a lot to do with how I chose to respond to the advice my parents hammered into my head. They took the things they learned about God through the Bible and their own experiences and taught them to me. I then had to decide whether these were the principles I was going to live by and put into practice.

When it came down to it, I realized I liked the way my parents had raised me and wanted to stay the course. I saw that they lived out what they taught us. When my parents talked to me about not doing drugs, it was because they believed it was wrong and didn't do it themselves. When they told me how important honesty was, I saw that they were consistently faithful to their word and commitments. Whatever rules my parents gave me, they followed them in their own lives. They are the type of people I've come to look up to and want to emulate. I know that they are trying their best to live lives that reflect Jesus' heart, and that's the kind of life I want to live too. They aren't perfect—none of us are—but they are good examples in my life.

I'm grateful for the strong values they instilled in me. But figuring out what made me who I am was something I had to do on my own; and, quite frankly, it's something I'm still working on. As I've gotten older, I've realized I need to find my own passions, define my personal set of priorities and boundaries, and decide whether I want to claim the faith I was brought up in as my own. But thankfully, my parents have provided me with a firm foundation.

CHALLENGES AND BOUNDARIES

Challenges to your values and boundaries come whether you live in the same town your whole life or move from one school to another. We moved quite a bit when I was younger because of my parents' careers. I had a mix of public and private education, and would go from schools with three hundred students to schools with three thousand students and then back. I found myself alone again each time, trying to figure out where I fit in. I tried to make friends quickly so that I didn't feel left out, and because of that, I would try to fit in or act cool and unlike myself. Then, I realized I was compromising myself and decided I'd rather wait for the right friends than act like someone I wasn't. Anytime my friends or people I knew would push me to do things like drink, smoke, or push limits with guys, for me, it was an absolute *no*. I wouldn't give in just because it was "cool." I've always been very hardheaded and stubborn when it comes to that, but being pushed to do things I wasn't comfortable with taught me how to use that hardheadedness to stand firm. And it took a long time to find people who accepted me for who I am and who were real about who they were. Not to say that I haven't made my share of mistakes . . . because, trust me, I have made tons of mistakes and still do. A lot of times, that's how we grow.

The situations that make you uncomfortable are the times you know you're being tested. These high-pressure scenarios force you to either own your values and stand by them strongly (and often publicly), or compromise what you know to be right and true, which usually leaves you feeling crummy. Remember that life is often about facing tough decisions. Being challenged. You have to be able to stand up for the things you believe in—especially when life hands you situations that can be tempting. Every time you take a stand and make the decision to do what's right rather than what might be popular, the adrenaline will start to pump inside you, strengthening your confidence. It's like saying no to that piece of chocolate that keeps calling to you—the more you say it, the easier it gets. You'll find that you don't need to do what others expect in order to feel good about yourself.

But it's not always about being tempted or challenged. There are a lot of fun ways to find out who you are and what you enjoy. Take the opportunity to try new and different things, whether that means hanging out with new friends, trying different hobbies, or even changing up your clothing and makeup styles. I never wanted to be someone I wasn't, but I had to branch out from my comfort zone too. That's how you find what *you're* about, not just what your friends are into or what the latest trends are.

Figuring out what made me feel good about myself helped shape how I present myself now. A lot of times, I went through my closet to figure out what type of clothing made me the most confident. One day I would wear a grunge outfit that consisted of leather pants, a moto jacket, some dark booties, and a studded black purse. The next day I would wear a preppy outfit that consisted of a collared shirt, a pleated skirt, and a pair of penny loafers. Sometimes I'd try sporty athletic wear, and other times casual jeans and a T-shirt. I would switch between softer, feminine looks and more edgy, rocker-girl outfits. I got a sense of what felt good to me by testing things out. The same was true for the makeup I tried. If I felt confident with the makeup I put on, I felt like Natasha.

TRACE YOUR FAMILY TREE

Begin with the basics. Write out the names of all of your grandparents, aunts, uncles, and cousins on a family tree.

Set up interviews. Make plans to sit down with as many family members as possible, especially the older generations, to ask them questions. You're specifically out to get biographical information about where they were born, the town they grew up in, what family lived nearby, and their religious upbringing. If needed, you can find more detailed lists of key questions and family tree worksheets online.

Share information. Chances are there's another relative in your family who is also interested in your shared heritage, so make your mission well known and try to work together.

Find a story and run with it. There may be one particular family story that you find fascinating, so use that as an entry point for research. Go to the library and look for old newspaper articles, and search the Internet to try to piece together the details of the event. All this work just may lead you to even more information about your family at large.

EMBRACE YOUR HISTORY

You can learn a lot about how your family came to be the way it is by looking at its history. Sit down with your parents, your grandparents, any extended family, and ask them about their backgrounds. In finding out about their struggles, hopes, and dreams, you'll learn about your connected family tree. Ask where your ancestors came from and learn more about their culture. I love sitting down and asking my parents questions about our family history. It makes me feel more in tune with where I come from and what my family history holds. It's especially interesting for me since my papa is from Russia. He tells me stories about his family's life there and where my last name, *Bure*, comes from. His side of my family lived a completely different life than we do here in America, and I love hearing about the culture he grew up in.

USE YOUR WEAKNESSES

It's hard to admit to yourself—or anyone, for that matter—that you have a weakness. We want to think we're strong enough to handle anything and mature enough to make any decision. But the truth is, we all have weaknesses. The question is, what do we do when we figure out what they are?

CHALLENGES YOU MAKE FOR YOURSELF

Not all challenges come from other people. In a lot of ways, we bring challenges on ourselves. Maybe you're like me and are naturally hardheaded, which has definitely gotten *me* into trouble at times. Maybe you like to find your own way of doing things, rather than doing them the way everyone else does. We're all different. And when we're trying to figure out who we are, we may do things or behave in ways that get us into bad situations.

Even though I've changed a lot over the years, some things are hard to change. Overreacting or acting like a drama queen is something I've always had to work on. Growing up, if my brothers annoyed me or said snarky comments, I usually reacted by yelling back twice as loud or provoking them in front of my parents to get them in trouble. Or if my parents told me something I didn't want to hear, like being told I wasn't allowed to have a sleepover at a friend's house, I would burst into tears and tell them they'd ruined my life, then hide in my closet assuming they wouldn't find me. I'm still working on this, and although I've improved, I can't say I won't ever be a drama queen again. Instead of using a stubborn and dramatic attitude in that way, I could have channeled my energy in a more positive and mature manner. If you are a passionate, hardheaded person, don't waste your time being dramatic about the little things that don't go your way. Use that fire inside of you to impact the world, a friend at school, or even a dream you've been wanting to pursue.

Besides, there's usually an upside to our flaws. Being naturally drawn to the dramatic gives me a depth of real feelings I can pull from if I find myself on stage or in front of the camera. As a performer, I have to be able to tap into my emotions at a moment's notice, and the more range I experience, the more I can find areas to relate to a character. As a songwriter, it also expands the scope of feelings I can write into my lyrics.

I'm also one of the most stubborn people I know. My mom told me that I've been this way since I was in the womb. She said that out of all her babies, I kicked and fought inside her belly the most. My mom likes to tell the story of my five-year-old self refusing to admit I made a mess with a candy bar in my room. There was evidence all over my face, but I simply would not admit to the truth. Lying to her was never the right choice. My parents have always taught us that lying is always worse than admitting a mistake. There will always be a lesser consequence and grace when you tell the truth. But my stubbornness will always be a part of me, and that's not always a bad thing. I just need to keep learning how to direct my stubbornness toward actions that will benefit me, like never giving up on my dreams and going the extra mile to achieve what I want.

TURN IT AROUND

There are parts of who I am and things that I have done that are hard to turn into strengths or positives. As a result, I've found it necessary to find ways to see the truth in what I do and how I feel from different angles and attitudes. Maybe for you that means talking to a friend, a parent, an aunt, or someone else you really trust. But there are times when you might be too embarrassed or just need to get something off your chest, which is true for me. So I decided to write.

I've kept a journal since I was fifteen, and I can't begin to express how much it's helped me. I was in the third grade when my mom first took me to Barnes and Noble to pick one out. It was turquoise and had "I can do everything through Him who gives me strength. Philippians 4:13" printed in gold cursive on the front. I was so excited to have my own journal—a private, personal space to write out my thoughts.

I still remember the first thing I wrote about. I had gotten in trouble for giving my parents a bad attitude and wasn't allowed to go to my best friend's sleepover birthday party. I was truly heartbroken, so I whipped out my journal and wrote all about it. It helped me get out my frustration. It wasn't until I wrote it out that I realized my attitude (whether good or bad) would always have consequences, and I needed to learn from what had happened.

HOW TO OVERCOME FEAR

Overcoming fear can be so hard. I suggest attacking the problem head-on. My biggest fear is heights, so one thing I have tried to do to help get my fear in check is challenging myself to face it. I have done several high ropes courses, jumped at the chance to ride thrilling rollercoasters, and try as many activities that involve heights as I can think of. All of this to prove to myself that it's okay to be up high! I'll be honest and admit that my fear is very much still there, but at least I have done things to try to conquer that fear. If you have something you're afraid of, push yourself to get out of your head and overcome it!

Take small steps. Don't feel like you have to take on the whole fear at once. Instead, set small goals to build your confidence and push your boundaries in stages.

Give your fear a name. Once something has a name, it's often easier to face because it's no longer an "unknown." It's a thing to be conquered. To add a little fun to it, give your fear a silly name—it takes away some of the edge, and may even help you laugh at the very thing you were afraid of.

Find support. Talk to your friends and family about your fear and let them know your plan to face it. I'm betting someone you love will take that rollercoaster ride with you. Every single fear-conquering activity I've done has always been with a friend. It helps me keep my mind off being scared, and I can just have fun because my friend is right there with me. Every time I've done a ropes course, for example, I end up almost peeing my pants laughing because my friends and I look so wobbly and unsteady. It's an easy way to lighten the mood.

Visualize. Take the time to close your eyes and slowly visualize a successful confrontation with your fear. If you're afraid of flying, imagine walking onto the plane, sitting in your seat, fastening your seatbelt, and then the slow, gradual takeoff. Keep yourself calm and breathe. This will help prepare you for the real thing.

Keep distractions on hand. Many times, you can overcome fear by using what distracts you. If you're at the doctor's office for a blood test and have a fear of needles, bring your phone packed full of funny videos, photos, music, and games you can play with one hand to keep your mind busy. If you're afraid of singing in front of large crowds, find one person in the audience or choose a point just above the heads of the people in the audience and sing your heart out to that door or sign. And as I said a couple points before, good company is always a great distraction, especially if your friends know how to make you laugh and take your mind off whatever it is you're afraid of.

Be patient. I'm still not over my fear of heights, but I continue to work through it. There's no timeline or rush to overcome your fear, so don't put that additional pressure on yourself to get over it *now*.

Celebrate even small victories. Acknowledge and feel proud of yourself when you make a small step forward. It makes the task of overcoming feel more doable and will encourage you to keep going!

A lot of times, when I'm upset, I still want to act impulsively and do something that probably isn't smart, whether it be yelling, throwing a fit, or saying a rude comment. But I've learned to take a breath and write out everything that's going through my head. That way I can transfer my thoughts onto paper and take a step away from the situation. This allows me to look at the scenario objectively and assess everything that's going on.

I wrote in my journal some years more than others, but it wasn't until I was in tenth grade that I really started utilizing it every day. Sometimes I even wrote multiple times a day about anything that went through my head. Writing it all down helped me understand how I was feeling and why. I could be honest without worrying about anyone else's feelings or opinions. I love going back to read old entries, reflecting on all the things that happened in my life. It helps you realize how much you've gone through, the growth you've made, the prayers that have been answered, and the things you can still be praying for.

REINVENT YOURSELF

Maybe it's a new school year or a new school, or you're just feeling ready for a change to become a better version of you. It's okay to want to mix it up and make some changes to the way you look or present yourself. Or to take it a step further and work on some negative behaviors that you're aware of, tired of, and outgrowing. Every couple of months, I like to clean out my entire room and closet, going through and getting rid of all the junk so I can start fresh. The cleaner and more organized the material items in your life are, the more you feel motivated to change internally too.

JOURNALING OUT THE FRUSTRATION

Slowing down in a stressful situation can stop you from saying or doing the first thing that comes to mind, and it can save you a lot of problems. One of the best ways to do this is by keeping a journal.

Writing down your thoughts and experiences each day will help you learn about yourself and how to deal with situations from a more levelheaded perspective. Take a step back and allow time to calm your emotions. It will help you react differently, and by taking time to write out your feelings you will hopefully make better choices the next time.

A journal provides:

A PRIVATE, SAFE PLACE. Your journal is one place that you can be yourself and explore your deepest, darkest fears and feelings. It's a safe way to express your emotions without fear of judgment or hurting others. Say what you have to say here. Let it all out.

ACCOUNTABILITY. Writing out your anger and frustration gives you a chance to unload, rather than lash out and regret it later. Once you have your feelings on paper, look it over and think about what parts would truly help you and the other person, and which words would be said just to hurt. Having everything there in front of you will help you see the difference and choose your words and actions more carefully.

CLARITY. As you write out your feelings and desires, you'll begin to understand yourself better. Don't edit what you write in your head before you put pen to paper. If your emotions feel big, it's okay to write big. If you are feeling small, it's okay to write small. Sit quietly and let it all out, no matter what you feel and what form it takes.

RELIEF: JOURNALING IS LIKE LETTING THE PRESSURE OUT OF A SODA CAN. There's so much tension, so much stress when you're angry or full of any other big emotion. Writing it all down lets you breathe again—even flop back in your chair or on your bed and flop your arms out.

A CONNECTION TO GOD. There is no one better to listen to your frustrations than God. The best part of writing them out for God's ear is that he can handle your biggest internal screams and your biggest questions. He's not going to be upset with anything you say. In fact, he wants to hear everything so that he can give you answers and direct you. God is always compassionate, always listening, always waiting for you. You may decide you want to write to God directly, which can be a more concrete form of prayer. It's a great way to form a stronger relationship with him as you contemplate your faith and religious questions.

Take some time to evaluate how you interact with people and what you like most about those moments. Love cracking up your friends with a joke or funny story? Then embrace your natural sense of humor and be willing to put yourself out there in conversations.

As you enter your teen years, it's natural to explore who you want to be. It can be a time of huge change. I know I've become more mature over the last couple of years, in part because I've heard lots of advice from my parents and put it into action. That's not to say I'm the most mature girl in the world . . . because I'm not. But I do strive to be that girl! I think exploring different sides of yourself within the parameters of godly wisdom is important during these transition years. It can help you see who you really are and the person you want to become!

> It's natural to explore who you want to be.

FINDING YOUR DIRECTION

Over the last couple of years, I've had to hone in on what I want to do with my life. I've asked myself questions about where I see myself in the coming years. What do I have to do to get there? I had to start planning ahead and making some tough decisions about my future.

I know that college gives you a time to discover yourself with a sort of protective security blanket, but without your parents totally running the show. Since I chose not to go that route, I've had to dive into adulthood faster than I realized. It's scary, to be honest. Some days, I still feel like I'm mentally fifteen or sixteen

TIPS FOR REINVENTION

Refresh your look. Go through your wardrobe and pull out the clothes that don't fit the "new" you, replacing them with a few new pieces that embody how you see yourself now. It's okay to let go of the old favorites of your childhood—you'll have room for *new* favorites! I always have the hardest time letting go of sweaters or shirts that I've had for so long, but at some point I need to make room for the new pieces that help me embrace who I am becoming.

Refresh your space. When you look around your bedroom, do you feel happy and energized by what you see? If not, it's probably time to redo your bedroom to match your current tastes. It doesn't have to be a big, expensive overhaul. Try simple tricks, like hanging a piece of beautiful fabric on an entire wall to give the space some texture and color. Replace the posters and artwork you loved when you were younger with more sophisticated or inspirational pieces. There are lots of places to find what you like within your budget—everything from eBay and Etsy to local garage sales and flea markets. Or try painting or making something yourself! Each year or so, I restructure how my room is set up and hang new paintings on the walls. It makes my room feel much more interesting and fun to be in—even something as small as changing the position your bed is in or moving it to a different part of the room can drastically change the appearance and overall feel.

Strengthen your character. Being respectful, showing your appreciation, and serving and caring for other people takes kindness and humility. When we put others first, we take the focus off ourselves (something we all need to do more often!), which in turn strengthens and builds our own character. While we're focusing so much on our own improvement, we can't forget that selflessness is one of the best ways to improve our perspective, heart, soul, and disposition.

Try new activities. If you know you need a change, nothing will help you hone in on what that is than trying new activities and meeting new people. Be brave and get out there! You'll get to know yourself in a new setting with new goals and challenges.

Write it out. Sit down with a pen and paper and envision your future and who you want to be. Write down whatever comes to mind in your journal. If you see yourself on stage, holding an acoustic guitar and singing your heart out, then it's time to ramp up those guitar lessons and sign up for your local open mic night or talent show. If that's really what you want for your future, put yourself on the best path to achieve it. Bullet point the exact goals you have. Don't hold back.

and in over my head. It's still hard to imagine being entirely responsible for myself, renting an apartment and living on my own—which is why I don't plan on moving out of my parents' house just yet. Other times I feel like I'm on a good path because I'm learning how to manage my time, schedule my appointments and performance classes around workdays and social activities, earn a living, and take over paying more than just my phone bill. It's all new to me and still a learning process. I'm realizing that it's one thing to find your direction, and it's a whole other thing to implement it.

YOU HAVE TO START SOMEWHERE

As I'm sure you've noticed by now, music is my passion. It's what makes me feel complete and full of energy. But that didn't just happen. When I was a little girl singing in church or in my room, I had no idea what a big part of my life music would become. But knowing your life's passion doesn't always start with an "ah-hah" moment. It usually starts with a bunch of "whoops" moments, and sometimes it starts with something you do all the time.

I started singing when I was very little. I loved to sing around the house. When I was about seven years old, I joined my school choir, something I continued to do throughout school. The first time I sang solo in front of people, I was going into sixth grade. We had just moved to California from Florida and we had found a new church to attend. At the end of the Sunday service, my friend Faith and I went into the youth ministries room so she could show me around. There was a microphone and piano set up on a stage. We started messing around, and she hopped on the piano and started playing the song that was on the music stand. I knew the song she was playing so I walked up to the microphone, which happened to be on, and started to sing. We jammed, alone in the big youth room. After the song ended, we kind of looked at each other and thought, *What just happened?*

It felt so good to create music together, and it was the first time I had ever sung in front of someone like that. From that day on, every single Sunday after church service, we would sneak into the youth room and play songs—Faith on the piano and me on the microphone. At one point we decided to create a set list of songs that we really liked to perform. We had asked our youth pastor if we could lead worship and sing a couple songs at our next youth group meeting. I think he was a little surprised, but he gave us a chance to show him what we'd been working on. We played a couple of songs, and he asked us to perform for the youth service that upcoming week. Soon enough, we began singing at school assemblies and other events. That's how I began to realize I loved performing. Two years later, I got the lead role of Ti Moune in my eighth grade musical, *Once on This Island*, which was a huge deal at that time. Since then, I feel this fire and thrill whenever I'm up on stage singing and performing. I want to do it forever, I really do.

I love singing because I connect with music on a level like no other. Music just makes me feel so much, on such a deep level. It's almost hard to describe how alive I feel when I'm listening to a powerful song, especially when I'm the one singing. Certain songs can make me feel so incredibly happy and others convey so much sadness. I think music makes me feel most in tune with myself. Performing allows me to share the beauty and power of a song with the audience. And it all started with playing around with a friend, a piano and mic, and a big empty room.

THE FUN OF TRYING

You have so many opportunities available to you, so follow your interests and explore! Don't put pressure on yourself to find "your thing" right away. There's plenty of time for that. As a kid,

I tried it all—lots of sports like soccer, volleyball, track and field, gymnastics, swim and diving classes—and some ballet and tap classes. Quite frankly, I didn't fall in love with any of those. I've tried different activities, including photography, painting, baking, and cooking, and even dabbled in DIY projects and crafts. There were so many things that I'd never tried and wanted to learn and experience—and I never knew whether it would turn into something I really loved! For example, I found that I loved

GET OUT THERE AND TRY NEW THINGS!

Leave your comfort zone behind and try new activities that push you to your limits and help you see what you're really made of. This is the best way to learn about yourself—your likes and dislikes. And there are lots of reasons why you should!

It can:

- Build confidence in your abilities as you put them to the test
- Create opportunities to meet new people and find those who will encourage you to be strong
- Challenge your mind as you complete new tasks
- Stimulate creativity in other aspects of your life
- Help you learn about your natural gifts and talents
- Offer a more fulfilling range of experiences and memories
- Inspire you to see the world around you as a place of adventure
- Connect you with even more opportunities to explore new things
- Who knows, the sky is the limit!

making home videos with my brother and learning about video editing. That's how I started my YouTube channel. I'm attracted to things that are creative and imaginative and these activities gave me the opportunity to express my creativity.

And you don't have to choose just one thing! After continuing to try new activities, I finally landed on tennis. I quickly became passionate about the sport and felt like I found my niche. I took clinics and private lessons several times a week, and practiced with my dad and brothers. I signed up for USTA (United States Tennis Association) matches and played tournaments on the weekends. I even began to dream about training hard enough to become a professional tennis player when I grew up. In high school, I tried out for the tennis team and made varsity right away, but during the summer before my senior year, I knew I wanted to concentrate on music, which was my first passion. Because of all the different things I've tried, I know that writing music and singing, things I truly love to do, allow me to be myself and enjoy who I am. It took time to discover what I really loved, and without trying new things, I might not have found it!

This is a time of incredible change for all of us, and it begins with getting to know the real you. From the time we enter elementary school to the day we walk across the stage, high school diploma in hand, most of us will change and refine everything from our activities and our friends, to our personalities and preferences. Embrace this time. Focus on what excites you, instead of what everyone else is doing. Try new things, explore the world at your fingertips, and who knows what you'll find out about yourself.

CHAPTER 2

EMBRACE THE REAL YOU

For you formed my inward parts;
you knitted me together in my mother's
womb. I praise you, for I am fearfully and
wonderfully made. Wonderful are your
works; my soul knows it very well.

PSALM 139:13-14, ESV

Practice makes perfect, right? So if you practice acting in a way that echoes who you are and who you want to be, it's going to stick and become second nature. They say it takes an average of sixty-six days to break a habit or create a new one. That may seem like *forever* now, but think of it over the course of your entire life, or even a school year. A little over two months is practically a trimester. That's nothing compared to twelve years of school. When you focus on being who you are and standing your ground for just a few short months, you'll naturally become closer to the person you were meant to be, no matter what circumstances you face.

Don't be discouraged if you struggle to show who you really are. It takes time. And mistakes will happen along the way. I'm human and make mistakes too. I've been there and done that! I haven't always represented Christ the way I should, but I try my best every day, learning from my mistakes and trying not to repeat them. And the only way to do that is to know what's good and right. And for me, I know those things by spending time with the Bible and having a relationship with God.

ACT WITH INTEGRITY

The bottom line is, you don't want to act two different ways—believing one set of values and principles, and then letting those go by the wayside when you're faced with adversity. That's like trapping two different people in one body. Be consistent. Ask yourself: Do my actions reflect my identity, my values, and what I believe in?

IS THAT REALLY COOL?

My Christian faith is incredibly important to me. I find my identity in Christ. But there are times when my actions don't reflect that, whether it's my choice of words, my attitude, or the way I present myself. When I look back at those moments, I wonder whether someone looking at me right then would have seen Christ in me. Would they see the person I want to be? Or would they see something else? Am I setting a good example for others, like my friends, brothers, or younger girls that look up to me?

There have been many moments in my life when I've done something and immediately regretted it. I'm a very impulsive person, which does not always lead me to make the best choices. In the moment, if something seems appealing, fun, or cool, I want to do it. Then I realize what I'm doing doesn't reflect who I am or what I stand for, and question, Why am I doing this? I've hung out with friends and gossiped behind another friend's back. In the moment, it seemed harmless, but later I realized how hurtful it was. I would hate to be gossiped about, so why was I doing it to someone else? There have been times when the words I said got out and ended up really hurting someone, even ruining a friendship. I've learned the hard way that if you say you are a true friend, you don't spread rumors behind your friends' backs. Take a step back and look at the actions of your life. Try to imagine what other people see in you, especially in situations that make you question your decisions.

BODY LANGUAGE

If you say you want respect from others, then don't wear clothes that cause people to want to look at you just for your body, rather than see you for the person you are. Flaunting your body in a non-classy way can promote ideas that you might not actually stand by.

Many of my friends do little photoshoots to post on Instagram. A lot of times, the photos are seductive or sexy, some-times trying to attract boys and other times to seem desirable. Once, a friend and I wanted to do a photoshoot of our own. We really loved re-creating dramatic photos, so when we saw some-thing impressive online, we wanted to duplicate it. In this case, the photo we decided to do was supposed to be an artistic shot of a girl in a beautiful ball gown, sitting in the bathtub. I was supposed to look like I was ready for this glamorous ball, but my makeup was running, my hair was damp and messy, and I was sitting in the tub with my dress soaking wet.

I was in ninth grade at the time, trying to impress the few followers I had on Instagram with my refined model shots. I loved to post photos that were unlike any of my friends' posts. When I uploaded the photos to my account, I was feeling really confident. Then, when my mom saw the photos, she sat me down and told me that although she loved the creativity and artistic edge to the photos, some people may view them as sexualized photographs because I was in a bathtub and wet.

I don't always have the insight my mom or a person older than me may have when it comes to what other people sexualize in their minds. My mom knew that wasn't my intention, but she thought it was better that I take the photo down. The last thing I wanted was to post something that could be taken as the opposite of what I intended, sending out a message that wasn't representative of the real me. I took the photo down right away and, although I was disappointed because I saw it as artsy and not sexy, I was glad my mom explained the difference to me. It's a lesson I'll never forget, one I understand better now that I'm a little older.

SO MANY WORDS

I know I'm probably going to sound like a Goody Two-shoes over this, but I've been taught my whole life not to use profanity. It was never allowed in our house, and still isn't. The first time I realized my parents were serious about bad language was when I called my brother a foul name using an expletive. My mom heard me and immediately brought me to the bathroom sink and washed my mouth out with soap. She said if I was saying dirty words, my mouth should be cleaned. Maybe this sounds harsh, but it didn't hurt; it just tasted gross and left a soapy taste in my mouth. Her point was made and I understood the importance of choosing my words wisely. And she usually followed up her teachable moments with a Bible verse to explain why the lesson was important.

It can be tough to watch your words. We hear people using profanity almost every day, even at school. When I went from being in a private Christian middle school to a public high school, I was hearing swear words *all* the time. After a while, my ears stopped perking at each word—they got used to hearing them in every conversation. One day, one of those words popped out of my mouth. I was talking with my friends, and when it happened, no one even noticed. It was so normal for everyone. I felt so weird and uncomfortable, and I immediately thought, "Wait, what? Did I really just say that?" My language was quickly deteriorating and I didn't like that at all.

I began to question what words really meant and why it was important. I wondered, *Is God going to hate me now that I've used swear words? I mean, I have so many friends that I consider to be good people, and they curse. Sometimes, it feels like you have to use those words to emphasize what you're talking about.* So what's the answer?

The answer is, God isn't going to punish me or stop loving me when I've done something I know isn't my best. In fact, God's grace covers all our sins, from the little ones to the big ones. But don't think that grace is an excuse to do whatever you want. God knows the intentions of our heart. So why is cursing a big deal? The Bible says, "Keep your mouth free of perversity; keep corrupt talk far from your lips" (Proverbs 4:24). We shouldn't let corrupt words come out of our mouths. This principle also relates to lying and slander. Even though it seems harmless most of the time, God tells us to avoid it for good reason.

FIND YOUR CONFIDENCE

I truly believe that confidence is one of the most important tools for success. Without it, how can you do everything that you want? I've always been a fairly confident person. I've never been super shy or turned off by new ideas or experiences, but my confidence takes a hit when I struggle with things I have a passion for, like tennis and singing. When I played in a tennis tournament and I didn't win an early match, my frustration would make it difficult to be positive going into the next match. I'd be focused on the fear of losing again. I always want to win and be the best at everything I do, but I have to remember that failure and mistakes are a part of life.

You can't avoid failure entirely, so what do you have to lose? If you don't fail, it means you never tried in the first place. It's better to put yourself out there and try. Having the confidence to try new things and being willing to fail at it is a lot more fun than living with fear. Fear keeps you from putting yourself out there and from really reaching for your goals, no matter how minimal or lofty they might be. Confidence means facing fear and not letting it keep you from your dreams. This is the same concept as bravery. Being confident means being totally okay with yourself and not avoiding an opportunity because you're afraid of being embarrassed. If I walk into a new experience and

PUT THAT JOURNAL TO USE

JOURNALING WAYS TO IMPROVE

There are always areas of ourselves where we can look more like Christ. Without reflection, it is easy not to notice these actions or bad habits. Should you give more and get less? Was there a situation you could have handled better? What could you do differently next time? Do you feel conflicted or guilty about anything? Write it down and think it through.

Document your victories as well. Did you control yourself when you normally would have totally lost your cool? Were you quick to hear, slow to speak, and slow to anger, as God calls us to be in James 1:19? Were you kind to others? Be honest with yourself. Take time to really dig deep. You change by first seeing what *needs* to change.

I fear that I might fail, then there is an increased chance I will. But if I am confident in myself, then I can attack the new experience head-on. And hey, if I fail, it's all a part of the learning experience. If I do great, rock on!

The same is true for areas in your life like your appearance. I've had to learn to feel confident about my skin. I've struggled with acne, and we will talk about it in more detail in chapter 8, but it's a huge struggle of mine. When I see beautiful girls with flawless skin walking around, and I'm feeling insecure about my troubled skin, my confidence plummets. I hate the way that makes me feel and how down I get about it. But when you look at the big picture, if you let all those tiny things of life get in the way of your confidence, you might never let yourself do anything and succeed. Be happy with who you are and be confident in the person God created you to be!

FAKE IT 'TIL YOU MAKE IT

You have the power to build yourself up with positive reinforcement and to practice confidence, just as much as you have the power to tear yourself down by comparing yourself to others and obsessing over your imperfections. These days, social media can play a big role in how we feel about ourselves. It can bring up your confidence like no other, and crush it like no other. It's a trip, I'll tell you that. A lot of people tend to base their worth on the amount of social media followers they have, how many likes they get, and how good their pictures are. But remember—social media isn't always reality!

So, how do you build your confidence? I say, "Fake it 'til you make it." To be completely clear, my gorgeous reader, authenticity is one of the most important qualities out there, so I'm in no way suggesting that you fake anything substantial about yourself, like your qualifications, your interests, or your experiences. But as you're building your confidence and working on positive reinforcements, it can help to act more confident than you may be feeling in the situation.

On *The Voice*, when I was singing in my battle round against Riley Elmore, I was very nervous. But I put on my sassy attitude and sang my little heart out. Was I actually feeling that confident inside? No way! I was jumping out of my skin with nerves, but I had to put on a brave front to get through the song with a strong performance.

Confidence means trusting in yourself, accepting who you are and what you stand for, and knowing that *you* are enough. It's focusing outside the fear and doubt so you can do your best. The more you tell yourself you will succeed and the more you build yourself up, the sooner that confidence will become a part of you. And if you find that no matter how hard you try, you aren't finding success, it may not be something you were meant to do.

> Confidence means trusting in yourself, accepting who you are and what you stand for, and knowing that *you* are enough.

Now we all know people who have never struggled with confidence—who are so sure of their special abilities that all you have to do is ask and they'll tell you just how great they are. Most of the time you don't even have to ask. You know the kind of

HOW TO BUILD CONFIDENCE

List your accomplishments. Make a list of the things you're proud of before bed each night, or at the end of the week. If you worked out consistently for the whole week, write it down. If you got a solid grade on a test or quiz, or if you got an internship at your favorite organization, write it down. The accomplishments don't have to be huge to celebrate them. It's important to remind yourself that you're working toward greatness, and it's always good to give yourself a pat on the back. Remember, you're able to do more than you think.

Don't compare yourself to others. Be proud of your accomplishments and pay attention to how *you* can improve, no matter what the people around you are doing. You have to run your own race, and, in the end, realize it's only against yourself.

Build up those around you. Give genuine compliments to your friends when they deserve it to help build a more supportive network. In time, this may very well become a support group. Whenever you're down, it's so helpful and relieving to know that you have a group of people who are going to support and push you. Find the friends you want building you up, and do the same for them.

Be kind to yourself. Talk yourself up, not down. If you find yourself starting to say horrible things about yourself, whether it's out loud or in your head, think about whether you would say something that mean to a good friend. If not, why would you say it to yourself?

Surround yourself with affirmations. Repeat truthful, positive, affirming thoughts by posting notecards with Bible verses on your mirror, and be actively involved in a Bible study you enjoy. Have a positive quote as a screensaver on your phone and computer. Have fun with sticky notes or positive coloring pages, posting them in your room, on the fridge, even in your car.

person I'm talking about, right? There's an important distinction between confidence and arrogance. Arrogance is being snobby, thinking that you're better than everyone else, and bragging about your accomplishments at every opportunity. Showing off and bragging aren't great qualities, and they can be very off-putting to your friends. Believe me. I've been around the entertainment business and I've seen the difference between arrogance and confidence, and it's not pretty. I've also seen others take confidence to the extreme and come off as very arrogant, though they may not have meant to. The secret is to build confidence in your abilities, but never forget to be humble and grateful.

CONFIDENCE GOD'S WAY

Building confidence in yourself and knowing you are truly valued doesn't just come from within yourself. We are beautifully made by God, and he has so much to say about how important we are and how we can build ourselves and others up. It comes in knowing what God says about it: "Do not be anxious about anything, but in every situation by prayer and petition, with thanksgiving, present your request to God. And the peace of God, which transcends

TIP **Moments of self-doubt.** The next time you begin to worry that you're not enough, or fears start to creep in, find ways to encourage yourself and others. Look outside of yourself. But more than anything else, base your value on the Word of God, not the standards of the world or your peers.

from all understanding, will guard your hearts and your minds in Christ Jesus" (Philippians 4:6–7). He also tells us, "For God has not given us a spirit of fear, but of power and of love and of a sound mind" (2 Timothy 1:7, NKJV) and "Cast all your anxiety on him because he cares for you" (1 Peter 5:7).

YOU THINK, GOD SAYS

What we think about ourselves can be based on what the world says; but wouldn't it be amazing if we only based it on what God says about us?

- You think, "I am too weak." God says, "I will give you strength."

    "I can do all things through him who gives me strength." Philippians 4:13

    "Though an army encamp against me, my heart shall not fear; though war arise against me, yet I will be confident." Psalm 27:3, ESV

- You think, "I feel alone." God says, "I will never leave you nor forsake you."

    "Be strong and courageous. Do not fear or be in dread of them, for it is the LORD your God who goes with you. He will not leave you or forsake you." Deuteronomy 31:6, ESV

- You think, "I am scared and anxious." God says, "Guard your heart and come to me."

    "Do not be anxious about anything, but in every situation, by prayer and petition, with thanksgiving, present your request to God. And the peace of God, which transcends from all understanding, will guard your hearts and your minds in Christ

Jesus." Philippians 4:6–7

"For God has not given us a spirit of fear, but of power and of love and of a sound mind." 2 Timothy 1:7, NKJV

"Cast all your anxiety on him because he cares for you." 1 Peter 5:7

- You think, "I am too tired." God says, "I will give you rest."

"Come to me, all who are weary and heavy laden, and I will give you rest." Matthew 11:28, NASB

"Therefore, let us draw near with confidence to the throne of grace, so that we may receive mercy and find grace to help in time of need." Hebrews 4:16, NASB

- You think, "I am unlovable." God says, "I love you so much, I sent my son to die for you."

"For God so loved the world, he gave his only Son, that whoever believes in him should not perish but have eternal life." John 3:16, ESV

"But God shows his love for us in that while we were still sinners, Christ died for us." Romans 5:8, ESV

You think, "Why should I bother?" God says, "Endurance brings great reward."

"Therefore do not throw away your confidence, which has a great reward. For you have need of endurance, so that when you have done the will of God you may receive what is promised." Hebrews 10:35–36, ESV

"The LORD will fulfill his purpose for me; your steadfast love, O LORD, endures forever. Do not forsake the work of your hands." Psalm 138:8, ESV

- You think, "I am worthless." God says, "You were bought at a high price."

"For God bought you with a high price. So glorify God with your body." 1 Corinthians 6:20

"And I am sure of this, that he who began a good work in you will bring it to completion at the day of Jesus Christ." Philippians 1:6, ESV

"Why, even the hairs of your head are all numbered. Fear not, you are of more value than many sparrows." Luke 12:7, ESV

- You think, "I am not pretty enough or I don't like [blank] about my body." God says, "You are perfectly and wonderfully made."

    "For you formed my inward parts; you knitted me together in my mother's womb. I praise you, for I am fearfully and wonderfully made. Wonderful are your works; my soul knows it very well." Psalm 139:13–14, ESV

- You think, "I am not smart." God says, "Wisdom comes from me."

    "For the LORD gives wisdom; from his mouth come knowledge and understanding." Proverbs 2:6

- You think, "I want more (or I am not content)." God says, "Be content with what you have."

    "Keep your life free from love of money, and be content with what you have, for he has said, "I will never leave you nor forsake you." Hebrews 13:5, ESV

PUT YOURSELF OUT THERE

Many people know what they want to do early on. For example, they've been singing and playing piano since they were three years old. Others don't find their true passion until they're in their twenties, or even later. It's all about the journey of trying a plethora of new interests and exploring what you love and figuring out what you don't love. You learn new things and see what you respond to the most. You also get to say that you tried it and know a little bit about many things. And some things stick with you. I still dance, do hip-hop, and play tennis. But once I found music, it just became my all-time favorite.

PUT THAT CONFIDENCE INTO PRACTICE

I can't say that performing on *The Voice* helped me get rid of all my jitters and anxiety, but I learned a lot about myself, my talents, and my decision to pursue music. It helped me grow. I think I'm always going to have the jitters before any performance. And I think some nerves are a good thing. But the experience showed me I want to keep improving my self-confidence. I know that I can sing and know that I have the ability to be successful at it. I just need to believe in myself, keep working on strengthening my vocals, and be proud of what I can do each step of the way.

Every time I take a small step toward my ultimate goal of being a vocal artist, I'm not only gaining experience, I'm gradually building my confidence. Things get a little easier the more familiar you are with those things you're good at. When you get more comfortable, you get more confident. The more confidence you have, the more willing you are to take the next step toward something bigger. Don't worry about failure, because it's bound to happen. If you were already perfect at something, you'd never need to practice in the first place, right? You'd never feel challenged; you'd never have that moment of victory when you overcame the ultimate obstacle. Practice makes improvement, improvement leads to overcoming, and overcoming grows your confidence.

> The more confidence you have, the more willing you are be to take the next step toward something bigger.

PUT THOSE GOALS IN VIEW

Making goals for yourself can be one of the most important steps in maturing and creating a life that is your own. If there is something you want to accomplish, write it down, verbalize it with friends and family, and begin working toward it. Don't put limits on your goals either. It could be as small as deciding to do twenty squats a day. It could be as large as becoming a producer of a hit television show. Putting limits on the things you want to do will only keep you from achieving them. And your goals don't have to be completed all at once. If you have ten main projects, don't be shocked if you haven't reached all your goals in one year. Some take time, and that's okay. As long as you're working each and every day to get closer to the finish line, it will all come together.

ACHIEVE YOUR GOALS

1. Write down your dreams.

This is a *huge* first step. Writing down your dreams—both big and small—is important, because you want to be able to actually see what your dreams are and visualize how you can achieve them. I love making a to-do list to get organized about what I want to do. There's nothing more satisfying than checking something off the list. You can reflect back and see all the things you've completed, and it's such a satisfying feeling.

2. Practice and prepare.

Practice makes perfect; it's that simple. You're never going to get any better at something if you don't practice. Make the time to really focus, with no outside distractions, in a quiet, comfortable space, and put together a plan for what you want to achieve each day. Invest time in your craft so you will become the best that you can be. It's not enough to be smart or talented or charismatic—you have to work hard and be prepared in order to succeed.

3. Succeed on your terms.

No two people are exactly the same, and no two paths to achieving goals are exactly the same. What works for a friend may not be right for you. The process of figuring out what you want and what you need to do to accomplish that goal is an important process. Whatever your dream is—from being CEO of your own company to being the next YouTube superstar—you have to start at the beginning with knowing who you are and what you believe in. Only then, when you really know yourself, can you achieve your goals on your terms.

4. Dream big, plan small.

Shoot for your big dreams (like making it on *The Voice*!), but start with small steps first. If you want to be a singer, take voice lessons, join the choir, and post YouTube videos. The baby steps are super important. Educate yourself in whatever your craft is. Take those small steps every day so that the main goal can be achieved.

5. Reward yourself.

Set milestones along the way that you can celebrate when you achieve them. For example, if your goal is to run a 5K, then the first time you finish a mile, you should celebrate! Never forget to tell yourself how awesome you're doing. And don't get down on yourself for not reaching your goals quickly. It's not always a race, unless you're running one, of course (and it doesn't start out that way). Be happy with how you're doing, especially if you're working your hardest and best.

TIP My family quote is "excuses are for losers." If you want something, work hard at it. Don't make excuses. Focus on whatever it is that you want to achieve and go get it. My dad calls it the loser attitude—if you make excuses, you are only setting yourself up for a loss.

TAKE THE LEAP

But it's more than just figuring out what you love. You have to do something about it. That's what putting yourself out there is about. Taking a leap of faith. Giving yourself a chance to succeed.

The reality of my goals didn't fully hit until a casting director who had seen my YouTube videos e-mailed me about auditioning for *The Voice*. To be completely honest, the initial answer in my head was no. I had watched *The Voice* since it premiered and loved the show, but I never had any desire to go on a singing competition show. I'm a very competitive person, and always thought those types of shows would get too intense for me. What if I didn't get first place? I'm not sure why I'm so competitive, and it's not necessarily with other people—it's more a competition with myself. But this time, I wanted to confront my fear of failing and let whatever happened happen. I'd never know if I didn't try, right?

The song that I auditioned with was "Can't Help Falling in Love" by Elvis Presley. Once I knew that I was going to sing that song for my blind audition, I was eager to start practicing. My vocal coach, Jason Catron, and I worked on the song together as much as we could through Skype and in-person sessions. I also had a lot of work to do on my own, including preparing my performance technique and connecting emotionally with the piece. During my blind audition, I was an anxious wreck. I didn't know what to expect when I was up there performing. Would any of the coaches turn their chair around for me? Was my singing voice up to par? Would I remember my lyrics or freeze up? I felt like a deer in headlights. So when the music started to play and I sang the first two verses, and Adam Levine pressed his button and turned around to face me, I was in shock! I thought to myself, *I made it!*

But after I heard Adam make his decision for Riley and not

me during the Battle Round, I was pretty bummed. While I was so thrilled for Riley (who had become a close friend), I also had to face the fact that I hadn't won. I cried a little bit—who wouldn't? But soon I realized that getting the opportunity to perform in front of four of the world's best artists, and with millions of people watching on TV, was an experience I'd take with me forever. I also knew that this experience was only going to open more doors for me in the pursuit of my musical dreams. Like I said, how would I know if I didn't try?

MAKE IT WORTH IT

Even though I didn't win the competition, I'm proud of myself for saying yes! I really put myself out there and worked harder than ever to follow my dream. So if you have a goal—no matter how crazy or unattainable it may seem—you have to go for it. Find the opportunities no matter how big or small to challenge yourself, and to take a step in faith to build your muscle memory, refine your skills, and get more confident with each one.

Something great will come out of a new experience, no matter what. You might not win or be the best at whatever you try, but you might learn something new about yourself that will propel you in life. If I hadn't taken a leap of faith and gone on the show, I would never have met some of my best friends, I wouldn't have been so fired up about performing and creating new music, and I wouldn't have gotten the opportunity to showcase myself. The experience doesn't always have to go as planned, but as long as you put your best foot forward, you can receive so much in return.

PUT THAT JOURNAL TO USE

SETTING GOALS FOR THE NEAR FUTURE (1–2 YEARS)

What are your biggest hopes, dreams, and desires? What is it that you want to achieve? Get started on smaller steps by jotting down realistic goals you can reach over the next year or two, then write out the direct actions you can take to get you there.

Do you want to achieve a major athletic goal, like being considered for a track scholarship for college? Start talking to the coaches at the college you want to attend. Find out what training or skills you still need to master to be considered, and write down your timeline benchmarks. Need to set a fitness or weight loss goal? Map out what it would take to lose one to two pounds per week with a new eating plan and workout schedule.

Reviewing your goals often in your journal will help you stay on track.

SETTING LONG-TERM GOALS (4–5 YEARS)

Writing out your long-term goals is just as important as the short-term ones, even if you can't check them off as completed in your journal each year. Where do you see yourself in five years? What would you like to accomplish by then? Do you want to have a successful blog or write a book? Do you want to get your degree?

Write out your college plan, with your major in mind—or perhaps two, if you're not sure—and your ideal timeline to accomplish it.

We can't predict life, and our dreams may change over the years. And that's okay! It's always good to see where you started and the new direction you're now taking; or you may need a reminder of what you originally set out to do. Keeping track of where you see your future will also help you detect the opened and closed doors God has set before you.

KEEP THE MOMENTUM GOING

When my time on *The Voice* was over, I didn't stop there. Right now, I'm working with a few producers to write and record songs, and I would love to come out with an EP—hopefully releasing one by the time you're reading this book. All I know for sure is that making music is what I want to do and what makes me happy, so I am going to continue writing, singing, and making music!

I still think about how it all started—singing with my friend Faith at our church's worship service. I now help lead worship for the main service of a church near my house, have performed on *The Voice*, as well as with the Grammy award-winning Christian pop band For King & Country on *The View*, at women's faith conferences, and, most recently, at the Honda Center in Anaheim, California before a sold-out crowd of 15,000 people. I'm blessed to have had so many awesome opportunities, from the big to the small, and I realize every experience counts.

If you have an experience or opportunity that heavily impacted you, use the momentum and keep going! Work harder than ever to use the knowledge and experience you've gained to reach your goal. But opportunities don't always land on your front doorstep like an Amazon Prime package. Keep the momentum going by networking, making contacts, and investing in relationships. You never know when the people you know will serve as instruments for your next step. Put in the work and don't let yourself become complacent or lazy. If you've achieved a goal, set a new one immediately so you can continue to build up your résumé or accomplishments. The sooner you get the momentum rolling, the more eager you'll be to keep on pursuing your dream.

CHAPTER 3

REAL FRIENDSHIPS

The language of friendship is not words but meanings.

—HENRY DAVID THOREAU

My best friend is the one who brings out the best in me.

—HENRY FORD

For most of my life, I didn't live very close to my friends. My schools were generally between a fifteen- to thirty-minute drive from home, so I didn't always have neighborhood friends I knew from class. Because of the distance, I rarely hung out with friends on the weekends, so I often opted to hang out with my brothers. We would build forts and tree houses, ride bikes, go on scavenger hunts, go exploring, and swim in the pool. We spent almost all our time outdoors—and who wouldn't in sunny Florida or California? All those years of playing with my brothers meant that I grew up as a tomboy, always ready to go play in the mud with the rest of the boys.

And even when I was younger, I didn't spend much time with girls who loved pink and glitter. I remember when I was in elementary school, all the girls in my grade were interested in things that I wasn't. I felt like I didn't fit in because I didn't have the latest Hello Kitty pencils and erasers—I just had regular yellow pencils. I didn't have the same pink Converse as all the girls in my grade—I just wore my tennis sneakers. I wasn't in the loop with what was "cool" in school because I didn't hang out much with those girls. I hung out with my brothers.

Now mind you, I recognize that all of these elementary school issues may seem irrelevant, but at that age, I really felt out of place. I wanted to fit in like all the other girls. I'd feel sad and lonely when I'd see a clique of girls hanging out and having fun and I wasn't a part of it. In fact, I was considered a "floater friend." Instead of having a consistent group of kids to eat lunch with, I'd move around table to table, floating from friend group to friend group.

I wasn't a loner—I could always find someone to talk to or sit with—but I really wanted to find my place. When I eventually did connect with a few friends on a regular basis, I learned that it didn't matter what I wore or that I had the right things. What mattered was what was in my heart: that I was kind and treated others with respect. As I got older and decided I wanted to make a difference in our world, it became clear to me that material things aren't going to make or break me *or* my friendships.

IMPORTANCE OF GOOD FRIENDS

Friendships are such a significant, enriching part of life, and that's especially true when you're a teenager. The best friendships build you up, make you feel like you can accomplish anything, and comfort you with the knowledge that you have a safety net of love and support if you fall or if you feel like your parents just don't understand. Often we spend as much time with our friends—at school, hanging out after school and on the weekends—as we do with our families. Friends can be a huge influence in our lives, both good and bad.

Good, supportive, healthy friendships are very important. Knowing that you're loved and accepted by your friends can provide encouragement for you to be yourself, try new things, and put yourself out there, even if you're afraid to step outside your comfort zone. What are friends there for but to laugh with you and remind you that you're not alone?

I've gone to a Christian sports camp called Kanakuk for the past three summers. I've made the most incredible friendships there, and they've been put to the test. Each cabin does a high ropes course up in the trees at some point during their stay. And as you know from chapter one, I am deathly afraid of heights.

We all had to partner up and go through the high ropes course together to build teamwork. It turned out that my partner, who I had gotten to know only a few days prior, also feared heights. But together we conquered the high ropes course without a scratch or a tear. We giggled the entire time, and we both encouraged one another to keep going, stay strong, and laugh off our anxieties. Instead of allowing ourselves to think about the height, we tried to joke around and make fools of ourselves up there. Had we not both been open to encouraging one another, that experience could have ended on a sour note.

When your friends believe in you, it helps you believe in your abilities as well, meaning the sky is the limit for what you can achieve!

YOU ARE YOUR FRIENDS

I also truly believe that who you hang out with is who you become. When you spend a lot of time with a friend or group of friends, you begin to echo each other's speech, mannerisms, and ways of looking at the world. I had a friend who used the word *literally* in every single sentence. (Okay, *almost* every single sentence.) That word wasn't even a part of my vocabulary before I became friends with her, and I slowly started noticing myself saying it much more often.

Are there any words that you've noticed your friends pick up from you, or vice versa? The key point is to pick up the good habits and not the bad ones. I've picked up poor habits as well, like using swear words or getting negative when people around me are negative too.

I had a friend in high school who I did *everything* with, from long afternoons hanging out after school, to shopping and listening to music, to sleepovers almost every weekend. She introduced me to her love for cooking. I got super into it, and we created new recipes and had bake-offs.

We became inseparable, and I started picking up some of her habits, like using bad language and embracing a more negative, standoffish attitude toward people. She wasn't a mean person, but her overall outlook on life was seeing the glass half empty instead of half full. In other words, she saw life through a filtered lens that darkened her surroundings instead of brightening them up.

I began to absorb some of that negative energy and started acting the same way. I didn't feel like myself and I wasn't the fun person I knew myself to be anymore. I hadn't entirely realized

HOW TO MAKE NEW FRIENDS

Whether you're attending a different school or a summer camp, or branching out of your circle, making new friends can be a challenge if you don't keep a positive perspective. Oftentimes, we're afraid of putting ourselves out there and getting rejected. To overcome those worries, try these simple tips for making new friends:

Be confident. When you're in a new situation, relax and smile. Remind yourself that everyone has to make new friends at some point.

Introduce yourself. Don't hesitate to go up to someone and introduce yourself. If you're nervous, chances are others are nervous too.

Ask questions. Get the conversation started by asking questions. Try talking about common interests like favorite movies or music. Coming from someone who has often been the new girl, making friends isn't hard if you're willing to engage. Try to relate on a topic at hand, and spark up a conversation.

Put your phone down. It's hard to make friends when you're bent over your screen, scrolling through the latest Instagram posts. Put it away and be present.

Get out there. Join clubs, sports, and groups you're interested in. Don't wait to be asked to do something—get involved! Following your passions will be fun for you and will help you meet people with similar interests. There are endless clubs to join, even online if you aren't able to physically attend one. A little research will go a long way.

the cause of my changing behavior until my mom told me she thought my friend might not be the best influence on me. I'm glad my mom picked up on this change, because it wasn't super obvious to me at the time. My friend was always nice and polite, and it's not like she pressured me to experiment with drugs or alcohol or anything I didn't want to do. But my inner-self was different. I wasn't acting as positively or happily, especially around my family.

I took a small break from hanging out with my friend 24/7, and it didn't take more than a few weeks to realize my happy self and positive outlook were coming back to me.

I didn't want to be rude or cut her off and tell her she wasn't a good friend for me, so I slowly distanced myself and found other people who were going to influence me for the better. A lot of times, I would end up staying at home with my family instead of going out with friends. I found that sometimes spending time with my family was the best option, because they could help me stay grounded and focused on good principles.

So I've learned to pick friends who will encourage me when I'm faced with decisions that may compromise my character. A supportive network allows me to have fun, but still know my boundaries and not be embarrassed if I have to say no to something. Without those kinds of friends, I would probably be in a lot of trouble with the wrong crowd.

If you are hanging out with a group of friends that have similar interests as you, who support the same things you support, and who want to live the same type of life you live, chances are those friendships will be strong and great! On the contrary, if you're hanging around the wrong crowd, you may find yourself in a tough situation. You may begin to get involved with

FRIEND SITUATIONS AND SOLUTIONS

SITUATION: Someone stole my best friend and I feel left out.

SOLUTION: Talk to your friend! We've all felt left out, and that's never a fun place to be. Be honest with your bestie and tell her that you want to spend more time with her. Don't be shy to open up about your feelings and how the situation is affecting you. Try to be proactive and include yourself in the situation as well. Don't sit at home waiting for others to invite you to places. If your best friend is hanging out with someone else, don't wait for them to text you the plans. Assess the situation and decide if you should ask to join them or hang out with other friends.

SITUATION: My friend and I both like the same guy.

SOLUTION: I have been in this exact situation. One of my best friends and I liked the same guy. We both knew that we liked him, but never addressed the issue because we didn't want there to be any tension. Finally, we both fessed up and talked about it. We decided that our friendship was WAY more valuable than a relationship with a guy who may not work out with either of us. We didn't want to throw away years of friendship over jealousy if one of us couldn't let go of our initial feelings. At first, it was hard because neither of us could pursue a date with him. But I'm glad we didn't because our friendship was so worth it in the end. Best friends are for life. Don't let a guy get in the way of that.

SITUATION: My friend is making bad choices, and I want to stop her from going too far.

SOLUTION: Being a good friend can be so much fun, but it also means having those tough conversations and being straight up. Your friend is lucky to have you looking out for her. I've had to have those kinds of conversations with friends before, when it felt like our friendship was moving backward instead of moving forward. I found my brave and told them what I saw and what my concerns were in the nicest way possible. This may not have been a comfortable conversation, but a good friend will appreciate you for being truthful in love.

And if someone comes to you with a loving concern, remember that while it's not always easy to hear something about ourselves we don't want to change, when you trust that your friend has your best interests at heart, it's smart to listen to her advice. Friends keep friends accountable. Being honest and gentle without overlooking valid concerns is a sign of a true friend.

SITUATION: My friends are gossiping about another girl and I don't want to be a part of it.

SOLUTION: Good for you. Remove yourself from the conversation. Don't feel awkward if you need to step away from a bad situation. One time I was at a restaurant with some of my friends, and there were things being said about another girl that weren't very nice. I was uncomfortable with the conversation and I felt like I needed to get a breath of fresh air and step away. So that's exactly what I did: I excused myself from the table for about five minutes, and when I came back, they were already on to a new subject. You can always walk away—or if you're feeling bold, you can speak up and tell your friends that nothing good ever comes from gossiping, and you'd rather not be a part of it.

SITUATION: I need to end a toxic friendship. What's the best way to do that?

SOLUTION: Don't be afraid. Sometimes friendships run their course, and ending the friendship is the best decision. You can go about it a couple ways: You can speak with the other person and let her know you think you should go your separate ways. You can also slowly start distancing yourself. No need to be rude or lie, but keep conversations short. Don't engage in as many details or overshare your life with her, and don't be as available to do things together. It's okay to make plans with other friends and not feel the need to include that person. The friend will usually get the hint and move on. But if a friendship ever starts to feel possessive and unhealthy, it's smart to share that with your parents or another adult.

activities that seemed innocent enough—like gossiping or telling little white lies—but bigger things are always right around the corner, like partying, stealing, and even drug use. Small steps usually turn into big steps that don't seem so big with time.

THE BEST KINDS OF FRIENDS

Everyone is different, and it's nice to have friends who come from different backgrounds and walks of life. I'm not suggesting you only hang out with people just like you. How boring! But at their core, good friends should share your values, such as trust, honesty, kindness, and compassion, as well as support you in becoming the best you.

That's particularly true during tough times. The world can be a stressful place, and we're often dealing with situations and

THE CHARACTERISTICS OF A REAL FRIEND

Trustworthy. You can share your biggest secrets and deepest-held fears with absolutely no chance they will become the talk of the cafeteria the next day.

Honest. When you need feedback, a real friend will tell you the truth, even if it's not what you want to hear.

Loving. In ways big or small, a real friend reaches out with an embrace, words, or acts of love to show how much she cares.

Authentic. A real friend does not hesitate to share her real self with you—flaws, mistakes, and self-doubts included—and will encourage you to do the same.

Supportive. A real friend accepts you for who you are and cheers you on as you set out to accomplish your goals, whether you achieve them or not.

Dependable. Despite busy schedules and other circum-stances, a real friend makes the time to be there for you, especially when you need it most.

Loyal. A real friend has your back, no matter what.

Encouraging. A real friend pushes you to be the best that you can be, whether that means trying out for the school play or standing up to peer pressure.

pressures that can feel all-consuming in the moment. Having a trusted friend by your side who you can confide in will go a long way toward feeling supported and heard.

For me, something that's important in a friendship is the willingness to listen. We all need to vent sometimes, and I want to be sure that my friends are going to listen to the problems I'm dealing with, whether or not they have advice for the next steps. In the same way, I want to be a good listener for my friends and let them know they have someone in their corner.

> Good friends should share your values, as well as support you in becoming the best you.

When I'm going through something in my life—whether it's a spectacular moment or a wobbly time—I love being able to share everything with my friends. They are there to comfort, support, push, and love me! I go to my friends with anything I'm going through, no matter how embarrassing, silly, small, or difficult. They have seen me at my worst and at my best, and they aren't there to judge me at all. I've had wonderful friends over the years, and I know some of them will be friends forever.

But there have also been times when friendships haven't been a smooth ride, particularly when I've changed schools or reevaluated my priorities.

During middle school and high school, I'd been attached to many different friend groups. Even now I love being friends with everyone because it allows me to connect with a wide variety of people. Having attended so many schools, I've gotten used to being the new girl and learning to spark up new friendships. Every person has a different story and personality, and it's exciting to see who you're going to click with. The one girl you saw on the first day of school, who you didn't think you'd be close friends with, could end up being a bridesmaid at your wedding. It's always a blast getting to know new people, to learn new things, and to get turned on to new music and TV shows.

In the end, I knew I found the right group of pals to hang with because I felt so comfortable around them. I felt like I could be myself and not worry about them pressuring me to try things that weren't in line with my beliefs. I didn't have to be so concerned about being tempted or being led astray because we all kept each other in check.

Now, I have to say I'm blessed with some of the best friends anyone could ask for. These beautiful, smart, supportive girls have my back no matter what, and are who I spend most of my free time with. They are truly like sisters to me. My best friends and I are so close that I can tell them anything. I trust these girls with my life. I met them all different ways, through mutual friends, at school, or through family. Some of them I've known for years, and others are new, blossoming friendships. Each of them care for me, challenge me, and inspire me. I cherish these girls with all my heart and love them endlessly.

I remember the first time things had ended with a guy who I had been talking to and really liked. I was devastated. I had just finished talking with him on the phone, and when I got to my room, I started bawling. I called one of my best friends, and before I even finished my sentence to try to explain what had happened, she told me she was coming over. She was at my house in ten minutes with cookie dough ice cream and my favorite wasabi snacks. We ate and talked. She let me cry and vent to her for as long as it took for me to finally catch my breath.

HOW TO BE A GOOD FRIEND

Listen. Sometimes we all just need someone to listen, even when we're obsessing or when there seems to be no good advice to solve the problem.

Be supportive. If your friend has a problem that you can help reasonably solve, do it. This could be helping her study for a midterm, picking her up from her after-school job, or making her soup and delivering it to her house if she's sick.

Give compliments. Sometimes girls can get competitive, but a true friend will always compliment your success.

Be honest. If there's something your friend is doing wrong, or if she's asking for an honest opinion, give it. Trust that your friendship is strong enough to take it.

Go with the flow. Sometimes friends get busy and need to focus on something else, like the lead role in the school play or an English paper they left for the last minute. Give her the space to concentrate on her priority-of-the-moment, knowing when it's over, she'll be back and ready to hang.

It meant so much that she was there to comfort me and alleviate some of the emotional pain I was feeling about the breakup. She was right there for me, no questions asked. I'm sure she had plans that night to go out with her friends from college, but she dropped what she was doing to be by my side. I couldn't thank her enough for being such an incredible friend.

With anything that we do—whether it be watching a sporting event, attending a musical performance, or going shopping—my friends are always encouraging and supportive of one another. We celebrate each other's small and large victories. I think I have the proudest group of friends, meaning that if any one of us has something big going on, the rest of us are always in the crowd, screaming the loudest. I'm so proud of all of my friends, of everything they've accomplished and who they are. I love that feeling of a tight-knit group of girls cheering on each other's every move.

I would hope that others see me as a great friend. That's not to say I don't have my moments when I make mistakes. I've had some trouble in the past with not picking the right friends. But I am glad I've found so many now who are always there for me, and who are positive and supportive. I want to make sure that I'm always that way for them. I hope you'll be that person for your friends too.

CHAPTER 4

REAL CONVICTION

For God has not given us a spirit of
fear, but of power and of love and of a
sound mind.

2 TIMOTHY 1:7, NKJV

So far, we've talked about finding and embracing the real you, and surrounding yourself with supportive relationships. But another part of the journey toward determining the best for yourself and for your life is being able to stick to your convictions. And even more, you have to know what your convictions (the codes you live by) are. There are tons of areas to look at, but first let's talk through some of the basics—the codes that guide your thoughts and how you see the world.

RESERVE JUDGMENT

It's very common to judge others. Sometimes we do it without even realizing it. We've all had that moment when we see someone or hear them speak for the first time, and a snap judgment about who they are and what they're about comes to mind. First impressions are meaningful in our culture, but that doesn't mean you should be close-minded after that initial take. The most mature and open-minded people immediately quiet that voice, and focus on getting to know the person first.

There have been many times when I've seen girls judge and tear each other down when people's backs are turned. In many cases, these girls are going through their own struggles at home or school and are lashing out because of their own insecurities and circumstances. In fact, in most circumstances, there is usually a bigger reason behind someone not being nice.

There are also times when I've been judged by other people, so I know how much it hurts. I get judged all the time on social media because of what I'm wearing, who my parents are, the poses I make, my captions, where the picture is taken, or which friends I'm taking it with. You name it and I've probably been criticized for it. And let me tell you, it's not fun to see the rude and mean comments. Who wants to see that? Maybe someone feels better about their own self for a moment when they put another person down, but I guarantee it feels so much better to be kind and give someone a compliment, rather than saying something nasty while hiding behind a computer screen.

Social media can be such a place of judgment, where people feel like they know you based only on the photos and content you post. As we discussed in chapter one, remember that's only one slice of life, not the whole picture.

I've had friends tell me that someone I don't even know was saying rude things about me. And then I realized, this girl thinks she knows me from social media! She had preconceived ideas about how I acted, my intentions, and my attitude based only on photos I had posted on my feed. Don't get me wrong, social media is a fantastic way to get to know aspects of someone's life, but it never tells the full story. I wish people would take the time to get to know me and who I am, rather than formulating their opinions about me from those small sections of my life they see on the Web.

My faith teaches me that it's not my job to judge and criticize other people, although I should hold close friends accountable if I see them making the wrong choices. If I'm out there judging everyone who passes by me, I'm not setting a good example of how to live a faith-based life. It's my job to be kind, loving, and to uplift other people. I want people to see Christ living in me, because I reflect the qualities Jesus did from the inside out.

Have you ever met a person who feels like a bright light? You feel a warm, generous, and loving spirit from them but think to yourself, *It can't be real. Maybe they're putting it on, because they can't really be that nice when no one is looking.* But you see the consistency in their life, and come to understand that it's the light of God within them—or, as the Bible says, the Holy Spirit. That's the kind of person I want to be.

DIG DEEPER

You never truly know what goes on in someone else's life until you reach out and ask. Every single person has a story and is on journey. So instead of making a judgment from afar, based on superficial observations or gossip, reach out and get to know the person. Find out who they are and what they believe in, and see how they treat others with your own eyes. We should all be given a fair chance to stand on our own merits.

I had a completely different idea of what one of my best friends was like before I really got to know her. I met her in Spanish class my sophomore year, and just watching her from across the classroom, I didn't think our personalities would match well. I automatically assumed we wouldn't be two peas in a pod before getting to know her. We then got paired together for a Spanish project, and after only two study sessions, we became very close. Her humor is my humor, and our personalities are a match made in heaven. You never know who you're going to click with, so be open-minded and don't rush to judge, even if you think you know what the outcome will be.

> Be open-minded and don't rush to judge, even if you think you know what the outcome will be.

Look for the basic goodness in others around you. Believe me, it's there in most people. And consider what our world, our communities, and even our high school cafeterias would look like if we all tried to find the good in each other instead of focusing on the bad.

We're all much more alike than we realize. We are all human, we all make mistakes, and we are all trying to navigate through life and find our individual path. All of our journeys are going to look a little different, but if we stick together and build each other up, the impact we could make could be huge.

Have you heard of the Kind Campaign? They are an internationally recognized nonprofit organization that brings awareness and healing to the negative and lasting effect of girl-against-girl bullying through their global movement, documentary films,

PUT THAT JOURNAL TO USE

JOURNALING FOR REFLECTION

Some people think that you have to be poetic, have a crazy-amazing life, or write about something super deep in order to journal . . . but you don't need any of that! You can simply write about what happened in your day or work through anything on your mind. It's nice to reflect on what my day-to-day life was like whenever I read my journal from years ago. We forget the simple and small details so easily, and sometimes those are the most cherished. Your thoughts and feelings will naturally leak into your journal entries, which helps you let out frustrations (as previously mentioned). It's interesting to see how much you grow while your life evolves from year to year. And what an amazing thing it will be when you are older and can see what you were doing that exact day ten, twenty, or thirty years ago!

in-school assemblies, and educational curriculums. Check them out at www.kindcampaign.com.

The bottom line is, when in doubt, be nice and keep a positive and open perspective.

DEALING WITH DRAMA

Oh, drama. We've all dealt with it, and despite our best efforts not to engage, we've all fed into it at one point or another. Your early teen years can be a wild time, with big emotions and raging hormones combined with a heightened desire to fit in with your peers. Not to mention physical changes that can leave you feeling a little off. All these factors can add up to a prime opportunity for drama.

I have experienced my fair share of drama. When I was in middle school, there were always little predicaments because of who was hanging out with who, and who liked who better. Looking back, it all seems very petty, but at the time it felt important. As I grew older, the drama would get more intense. If someone lied or did something shady, a whole friend group had to get involved, and everyone would assess the situation, choose sides, and create even more drama. Sometimes this even meant that the situation was misunderstood and rumors were spread.

Gossip is so common, and it's one of the biggest sources of drama in any high school—and in life, for that matter. We see things going on around us and we talk. We share our opinions and thoughts, not always with malicious intent, but it can be easy to say hurtful words.

My parents have always told my brothers and me, "If you don't have something nice to say, don't say anything at all." Try putting this into practice. If you have a negative thought about someone, write it in a journal and pray to God about it. Don't bring others into a situation that could turn into a gossiping group chat.

When I was in eleventh grade, there was a girl at school who I shared some mutual friends with, but didn't know really well. I heard from my friends and other people around school that she wasn't talking very highly of me. I was hurt—how could she say these mean things about me if she didn't even know me?

I can be a very confrontational person when it comes to these type of situations, and I wanted to nip the drama in the bud. So I got the girl's phone number and called her. I explained I just wanted to clear the air between us since I had heard some rumors. She told me that she had heard that the same things were coming from me about *her*, which was definitely not the case. By the end of our conversation, we learned that one of our mutual friends had misspoken and started all this miscommunication. We cleared the air and she became a good friend of mine. We both learned that gossip and drama are unnecessary

PUT THAT JOURNAL TO USE

PRAYER JOURNALING

Praying is a vital part of growing in your faith, whether it's to ask for help with a problem or to tell God thank you for being there. However, we all know how fleeting and distracted our minds can get. One way to spend quality time in prayer with our Heavenly Father is to sit down with a journal. Prayer journaling is such a fruitful activity when it comes to your prayer life. It will help you get all of your worries and fears to stop swirling around in your head and start flying up to the hands of God! Write your prayers specifically, and don't forget to mention what you are thankful for as well. Look back at your journal often to update it. It's a wonderful thing to be able to see what prayers God answered (or some he didn't that you now see was for the best).

when you can spend your time having honest conversations and open communication.

Gossip has long been a part of our lives, but it is even more dangerous today than ever before. E-mail, text messaging, and social media all mean that negative statements about someone can live forever online. It's also so much easier to hide behind a screen if you want to say something ugly about a person. You don't have to face your target and see their reaction right in front of you.

Think about what a positive world we could live in if everyone stopped gossiping. It may sound idealistic, but each of us can make a difference. Even if your choice to keep your thoughts to yourself only affects your immediate peer group, that is worth the effort. Remember that many small changes add up to big ones. Be the person who walks away when your friends begin to chatter about someone else. The more you stand against it, the more people will follow your lead.

STANDING UP TO PEER PRESSURE

Peer pressure can come in many different forms. Of course, we're all familiar with the stereotypical pressure at parties to do drugs, to drink, or to have sex. But there's so much more to the daily pressures we face than those scenarios. It's hard to stand on your own with confidence. You're still getting to know yourself, figuring out what you believe in, and developing the tools to make decisions that are authentic and represent you well. (Shout out to the hard work we covered in chapter 1!)

There are always going to be social situations that are difficult to navigate. If someone wants you to do something that you're not comfortable with, say no right away. Most people will respect you more for your convictions than make fun of them. And there will be times when you don't realize that you've been the extra push someone needed so that they'll have the courage to say no next time too.

When I was in eighth grade, I went to my friend's birthday party at her house down the street from mine. We hung out, ate some cake, told stories, and were having a great time. I was with my friend Faith, the one I started singing with at church, and toward the end of the party some other girls showed up with alcohol and weed hidden in their purses.

I told Faith that I didn't want to be put in a situation like that, and neither did she, so we said our goodbyes to the birthday girl, thanked her mom, and left. Simple as that. I don't know if anyone at the party ended up drinking or smoking, but I didn't want to be offered anything illegal and risk getting in trouble for something I didn't want to be a part of the first place.

I didn't need to stand there and point my finger at the girls who brought the drugs while reading them the riot act. Trouble usually finds a way of exposing itself without our interference. Instead, I just chose to remove myself from the situation. How easy is that? If you're ever around someone who is doing something that goes against your principles, you always have the choice to simply walk away.

Of course, drinking and drugs are the most common forms of peer pressure you can combat. But peer pressure can take another form when it comes to your daily social interactions. Everyone wants to have friends and feel included in a social circle, and oftentimes that comes with the idea of "groupthink," where everyone dresses, acts, and thinks the same. This all stems from the powerful pressure to fit in and be accepted.

But remember, as good as it might seem to be popular or fit in, it feels even better to be appreciated for who you really are. The power of influence from your friends is not necessarily a bad thing if you have friends who are making good decisions and support you in doing the same. In that case, their presence may help you to stay on track.

All of us just want to be loved. We want to feel like we belong, and a lot of times we do that by trying to dress like everyone else, act like everyone else, and do whatever it takes to "fit in."

No one wants to be the odd man out, but I think it's awesome to be different. Be unique. Most importantly, be yourself. Don't worry about fitting into someone else's version of "cool." There have been times when I have wanted to fit in with certain people. I admit it. When I was in middle school, for example, my group of friends would always wear their school uniform exactly the same way. I thought that if I didn't coordinate with them and wear the same white Converse shoes, the same plaid skirt with black leggings underneath, and the same gray hoodie, I'd feel like I was out of the group. But as I have grown older and learned better, being my own self is much more satisfying.

FACING CRITICISM

How you handle feedback and criticism says a lot about your character. I have struggled with accepting criticism gracefully myself. I can get pretty defensive, and hate feeling like I did something wrong—and usually criticism is all about how you can do things better. I have had to learn to take the advice I'm getting and use it to my advantage, strengthening my skills by listening, and applying tips when the criticism is constructive. We can *always* improve what we are doing.

I used to struggle anytime my parents gave me criticism, whether it be in sports or acting. My papa was my tennis coach for a very long time, which meant he would always give me advice and critique me on things I could do better on the court. That was his job as my coach, but I took it personally and very hard, usually resulting in tantrums and lots of tears. Anytime I had auditions, my mom would be the one giving me advice and helping me with my acting. I felt like I couldn't do anything right and I would get so upset. I remember my mom telling me that if I don't get the advice, how can I get better? Now, I try my best to use the constructive criticism that I receive to improve my skills.

The same was true for me on *The Voice*. A large component of the show is giving the artists feedback so their performance can improve. A lot of the advice I was given involved things I already knew, like singing with confidence, being in the zone, opening up my voice cavity to its fullest extent, practicing each and every day, and treating my voice with the utmost care. It was a matter of putting those comments into action, which can be difficult on such a huge, public stage. I had to work on being confident in my abilities and not letting my fears get the best of me. After I was eliminated, I thought, *It's only up from here.*

DIFFERENCES

Looking back, I wish that I had never felt the need to fit in. I could have been dressing up my school uniform with my own sense of style all that time. Now, I don't worry about things like that anymore. I wear whatever my heart desires and what I feel best in. I share my opinions, whatever they may be, and I don't feel like I need to say certain things to get my friends to like me. My friends and I all embrace our differences and preferences. That doesn't mean we don't question each other's quirks. We do. But those differences are what make you, *you*. If I think black leather pants are stylish, I'll wear them even if my friend thinks it's a fashion no-no. If my friend wants to dye her hair pink, she should go for it even if I would never want to. These are the types of things that make us individuals and one-of-a-kind.

Social media is where a lot of people get stuck on "what is cool." When we look at Instagram models, celebrities, or influencers with huge followings, we often want to do exactly what they do. It looks so cool! You might think, *Well, if they're getting thousands and thousands of likes for dying their hair electric blue, should I be doing the same?* I'll admit I'm totally a victim of this. If I see something I like on a popular Instagram page, I want it. I feel like if I don't have it, I'm not keeping up with what's trending. It's easy to let comparisons overtake our lives and we begin to focus only on what is going to make us popular.

Embrace your individuality and autonomy as much as you can. There's no doubt that your friends will be among the biggest influences on you your entire life—no matter how independent you may consider yourself.

Don't let others affect what is unique to you and makes you who you are.

CHAPTER 5

REAL TALK ABOUT GUYS & RELATIONSHIPS

Daughters of Jerusalem, I charge you:
Do not arouse or awaken love until it so
desires.

—SONG OF SONGS 8:4

Love is an irresistible desire to be
irresistibly desired.

—ROBERT FROST

My first kiss wasn't the stuff you see in fairy tales. It was on the night of the eighth grade musical. We were performing the Broadway Show *Once on This Island*, and I played the lead character, Ti Moune. I had to get to school extra early for some additional rehearsal and to get into my costume and makeup.

While I was waiting, I was texting with a boy I liked. I told him that I was at school, waiting to get ready. He told me he was going to come early too because he wanted to talk to me. I sprinted over to a couple of my girlfriends who were in the room next to me and told them everything. They all started freaking out for me and said, "He probably wants to kiss you!"

Of course after they said that, I got totally nervous. *How am I supposed to kiss someone? What if I'm a bad kisser? Am I even ready for this?* When he got to the school, he immediately grabbed my hand, and my heart started beating so fast. We walked hand-in-hand all the way up to the school's playground at the top of the hill.

I was so nervous, I started to walk really fast, and ended up kind of walking in front of him. He said something I didn't hear, and I quickly turned around to try to understand what he had said. As soon as I turned around, our faces were directly in front of each other's, only leaving about two or three inches of space between us. Next thing I knew, we kissed. I had gotten so nervous that when I turned around and his face was close enough, I just pecked him!

Afterward, I was mortified, and I was thinking to myself that it wasn't a wonderful first kiss. I had imagined my first kiss to be special, and this one had been just blah. When I looked at my phone, I saw that my teacher had texted me to come back to start getting ready for the show. I told my crush I had to go, and he started to lean in for another kiss, but I did *not* want to kiss him again. I didn't want another embarrassing moment. So I moved away and said, "I'll see you there!" How awkward!

If you think that's embarrassing, my second kiss was worse. Later that school year, I was at our eighth grade graduation party with the same guy at our classmate's home. There was a movie theater room inside the house, so our entire grade was planning to watch a scary movie. I wasn't a fan of scary movies then and still am not. Those of us who weren't interested in the movie sat in the back of the room and talked quietly while the rest of the kids watched the screen.

So there we were, me and this boy I liked, sitting together and talking, when he leaned in for a kiss. This time, I felt more comfortable and it was a lot less awkward. Well, until my *entire family* walked in!

The door to the darkened theater room opened, and as the light streamed in I could see my papa, my mom, and my two brothers staring at me. I was mortified. I immediately got up and pretended like nothing had happened. I could see that my papa was very, very angry, and he said sternly, "Let's go." Talk about a silent and uncomfortable car ride home. My brothers didn't even tease me, because we could practically see the steam coming out of my parents' ears.

My parents never really sat me down or talked specifically about the incident like they usually would when I did something they didn't approve of. Probably because they knew the sheer embarrassment alone had been enough.

They did tell me later that while they were teenagers once and understood the growing curiosity of physical relationships, they were disappointed to walk in on me like that. Simple kissing can easily and quickly lead to more, and that was something I'd already made a commitment to God not to do.

BE YOURSELF

We live in a world that seems to revolve around sexuality. What happened to good old-fashioned crushes and dating? Well, thankfully, we're part of a generation of young women who are empowered and educated, and so able to take control of our love lives. That's right—girls can absolutely take the first step to get to know a guy, and feel confident in setting the pace for their relationships. And, yes, you can also abstain from dating altogether to focus your energy on your goals. Either way—or somewhere in between—you're in the driver's seat and that's a good place to be. So sit back and be yourself as you navigate the twists and turns of the road that is dating and relationships.

That's easier said than done, of course. In chapter 1, we talked about the importance of knowing who you are and the ways in which you can work to really know your true self. But when it comes to interacting with members of the opposite sex, sometimes all of that knowledge and self-assurance can fly right out the window. Trust me, I know firsthand.

This is the story of my life. I don't understand how it happens, but I literally forget how to formulate a sentence properly in front of guys I like. During my senior year in high school, I was sitting with a guy I had a crush on while doing some math homework. He was trying to make conversation, and asked me what the homework was about. When I tried to answer his question, what I said wasn't even in English. I have no idea what language came out of my mouth; it made absolutely no sense. I quickly played it off and restated the sentence I had hoped would originally come out.

Obviously, when you like a guy, you're going to get flustered. Clearly, I was *very* flustered. It's not always easy to act natural when you're face-to-face with your crush. But take it from me and try to be yourself, even when the adrenaline of being near your crush makes your head spin. If you find yourself getting nervous and jittery, try taking a deep breath before speaking to help calm your nerves. Or, focus on someone else in the group instead of him. Remember, he's human too.

TALKING TO GUYS

Ready to strike up a conversation with your new crush? Use these tips to get to know him better and even put your feelings out there!

Be outgoing. If you want to talk to a guy, don't be shy. If you're at school, try asking him a question about the assignment, or even to borrow a pencil. Just get the ball rolling, and next thing you know, you're in a conversation!

Keep the conversation light and fun. If a guy enjoys your conversation, he'll want to keep talking. Find a common interest between the two of you to keep your conversation flowing, or ask him about something that he's super passionate about. If he's on the baseball team, ask him how it's going or even when the next game is.

Smile. Body language says a lot about how you're feeling. People are attracted to people who smile, so start there. Then work on the rest, especially the way you stand. Don't cross your arms, which says, "Don't approach me!" Instead, face out into the room with an open posture, showing you're open to conversation.

Be yourself! Ultimately, you want a guy to like you for you. So don't pretend to like bands or movies you're not interested in. You can be open to something new, but don't compromise who you are.

Of course, it's not always nerves that cause some girls to act differently around boys. Some girls act differently because they want to impress a guy or seem cool in front of them. I am totally guilty of doing this. In fact, I have completely changed the way I would normally talk to guys in an attempt to make myself seem more sophisticated. Normally when I'm around guys, I'm a dork. I like to have fun and laugh. I'm never focused on trying look cool or sexy, but oftentimes I think, *Maybe if I tried doing that, boys would notice me more.*

Most of the time it actually ends up backfiring, at least for me. It happens anytime I purposely try to look cool in front of anyone, for that matter. I look so unnatural and come off as ridiculous.

It goes both ways too; boys aren't always able to be themselves around girls. Think about traditional stereotypes for girls and guys—guys still think they have to be tough and macho, and often show off in front of girls. It's not always easy to tell what a guy is really thinking.

In the big picture, I can't stress enough how important it is to be yourself. If a guy is interested in you, you want to know for sure that he's really interested in *you*, not some exaggerated version of yourself that you put out there to impress him. If you are yourself from the beginning, you don't have to worry about trying to change yourself later. Don't say you love the LA Kings and video games if you never watch sports and can't tell the difference between *Call of Duty* and *Super Mario Bros.*

IN HIS HEAD

If I could master one thing about relationships and boys, it would be figuring out what boys are thinking. Boys can seem so complicated, but at the same time not complicated at all. I'm sure they think the same about us girls. I'm always scared that I am overthinking what they're saying and that I'm going to read them wrong.

If you're like me, my advice would be to figure out what type of personality he has and how he usually talks and conveys his feelings. For example, if a guy is super sarcastic all the time, keep that in mind when talking to him so that you'll understand his humor, or when what he says is actually a joke. If a guy is super straightforward, then you know what you're getting. It's all about vibing with the person you're talking to. This goes for having a conversation with anyone.

In eleventh grade, I had a crush on a guy who was a year older than me. Sometimes he was flirty, other times just friendly. I could never figure out if he liked me or if he thought I was just a friend—and it bugged me. I remember reading into everything he said to me, in all forms of communication. I feel like if I had just let things play out, instead of overanalyzing everything, it wouldn't have been as stressful to figure out his intentions.

Sending signals to guys can be difficult for me too. Sometimes if I playfully tease and joke with a guy, it could go too far, to the point where they might not think I'm into them. I have to be careful with the way I come off. Other times, my friends have been so flirty that it turned the guy away. I say the best advice is to take things slow. Work on developing good rapport and a friendship based on mutual likes and dislikes. Then it's much more natural and comfortable to take things to the next level.

Dating can be a thrilling opportunity to connect with someone else, have a lot of fun, and even learn more about who you are in the process. But don't feel pressure to find "the one" right away. It can be a struggle to have a relationship and worry about someone else when you're still trying to figure out who you are. You probably have big plans for the future—to go to college and/ or pursue your dreams—so if you are in a serious relationship, be sure your significant other will support your dreams, not replace them. Enjoy yourself, but don't lose yourself and get caught up in the excitement and emotions of a relationship they may distract you from your future goals.

One of my favorite talks is about purity, and it's given by Joe White. He speaks at a camp called Kanakuk, which you'll read more about in chapter 9. Joe talks about how valuable we are and how fragile our hearts can be. Oftentimes, I get discouraged when it comes to guys, especially because I'm not currently in a relationship. Joe speaks about how we are meant for one person, and we shouldn't give ourselves up to someone who hasn't put a ring on our finger. At the end of the night, he gives each person a penny that has never been touched. It is pure and clean. With the love of Christ, we can be washed clean of our sins and be pure and born again. I've heard the same talk three years in a row, but I never get sick of it.

TIP **Don't do anything you don't want to do.** It's better to say no in the moment than to later regret something you've done. Saying no is never bad. Trust your instincts, and don't give in to pressure. You wouldn't want to feel bad and get down on yourself for the decision you made—that's the worst. It's important to stay true to what you stand for and represent.

BE PATIENT

You don't need a boyfriend. Yes, that's right. Say it with me: *I don't need a boyfriend.* I have to remind myself of that quite often, because there's so much pressure to couple up if it seems like all of your friends have found their matches. But let me tell you, you can have just as much fun by yourself, with your best friends, focusing on doing exactly what you want to do. Live your life and focus on your passions and hobbies.

Honestly, I know it's tough to wait for the right person who shares your values. In my eighteen years of life, I've never had a boyfriend. I've exclusively talked to a couple of guys I've liked a lot, but I've never really taken it to the next step of having a real relationship where we called each other "boyfriend/girlfriend." I simply haven't met a guy I've been interested in who shares my faith and values. It's not worth it to me to date someone who isn't like that. I think that it's okay if I don't find the boy of my dreams right away, though it's a tad bit annoying that I haven't found him yet.

It's not easy seeing other people in relationships while I'm not, but it's going to make the person I end up with so worth the wait. For me, the point of dating is to find a husband. I feel like saying that might freak some of you out. But if I don't believe in casual dating or casual sex, why would I want to date someone who I couldn't potentially see living the rest of my life with?

There have been a handful of guys I have had a crush on and I later realized were not the right match for me. I would start talking to a guy I thought was super cute, get to know him, and find out that we just weren't meant to be together. That can be a bummer, but it's all about learning and knowing what you like and don't like in a guy.

LIST: TOP 10 REASONS IT RULES TO BE SINGLE

1. You have time to do everything and anything you want.
2. You're able to focus on your passions.
3. You have time to plan your future and work toward your goals.
4. You are able to focus on God and devote more time to him, which shifts your priorities.
5. You'll be ahead of the game by learning from your friends' relationships.
6. Your independence grows as you do activities alone.
7. Your relationships with friends and family strengthen.
8. You save money by not paying for dates or buying gifts.
9. There's no boy drama!
10. You'll be ready when the right person comes along.

FRIENDS FIRST

I'd suggest building a solid friendship with someone before beginning to date. You really want to get to know a person before rushing into a relationship. Although physical attraction can be very strong and a key part of a relationship, you need to know the person you're about to date. Once you build a friendship, you'll get a sense of their intentions, what they're like, and what they stand for.

Building a foundation of trust before making any relationship a romantic one will help you to feel comfortable and empowered. You already know he loves your sense of humor (so joke away!) or that he appreciates your nerdy obsessions (no need to hide your sushi-printed clothing collection). Doesn't it sound great to be yourself? This also applies to boundaries. If a guy is expecting sex from you but you're waiting for marriage, the relationship isn't balanced in the values you share. If you are

DEFINE THE TERMS

Different geographical locations have a different way of expressing the dating terms listed below. If you live in California, the meaning of something might be slightly different than if you lived in Texas, Maryland, or Florida. Age also matters. My mom will say the definition of a word is one thing, and I have to explain that's not what it means *today*. But while it all depends on where you live, what generation you come from, and the slang you use to define your relationship with someone, here are some of the basics most people can agree on:

Official: You are dating someone. You call them your boyfriend or girlfriend, and vice versa. You are an official couple.

Exclusive: You both have expressed your feelings to one another, and you both understand that you don't like anyone else and aren't talking to anyone else in the same way, but you aren't putting the "official title" on anything.

Talking: Similar to exclusive, in that you both have expressed a mutual attraction and you both want to spend time together, but this is a little less intense. You're still talking to others to see if there's a connection there. There are no titles or an official relationship. It's more like a crush that you can get to know.

both on the same page as far as physical limits, you won't have to worry about being pushed to do something you don't want to do.

Group dates are an awesome way to build a foundation before you date someone. It's a great way to get to know someone casually at first, because we're all much more comfortable in a group than going out solo anyway. Make group dates fun too. Go to an amusement park or mini golfing! There are tons of things you can do in a group setting.

> Building a foundation of trust before making any relationship a romantic one will help you to feel comfortable and empowered.

If you have a crush on a guy but you're too nervous to go on a date alone, bring another couple, or have his best friend and your best friend come along. Simple as that! I know that I'm most comfortable when I'm with my best friend. I feel like I have little bit of a safety net when she's with me. She has my back if something is going wrong, or if there's a lull in the conversation. If I do feel like I have a connection with the guy and things are going well, then for sure, a solo date would be awesome next time. Then I can get to really know the guy better when it's just the two of us.

TECHNOLOGY AND DATING

Social media, texting, and other online platforms have changed the way we communicate, and that's especially true when it comes to dating. When developing a relationship, texting can be helpful to meet someone or set up plans, but it's not the way to make a real connection. Hanging out in person, no matter how you initially meet, is the best way to really get to know someone and develop a relationship.

The same goes for social media. Instagram, Twitter, and other sites can be great places to meet people. In fact, a relationship I had with a guy last year all started through Snapchat. He had posted a photo of his new puppy on his Snapchat story, and, being the avid dog lover that I am, I snapped him and asked all about his new puppy. At the time, I was more interested in that adorable pup than in him! We started texting and talking soon after, and then began hanging out in person. We ended up being exclusive for a little while. I think a lot of people nowadays are meeting through social media, with it being such a huge part of our generation and world.

While it's so common and often fun to meet someone online, it's super important to take your relationship off the screen. As I said, social media platforms like Instagram, Twitter, Snapchat, and Facebook are all great ways to get a sense of what the person is into and what they could potentially be like. I think it's totally fine to meet someone that way, but once you meet them, it's best to take the majority of future communication offline.

Social media can also be misleading in all sorts of ways, and if you're in a relationship, this can be particularly tricky. Subtweeting can lead to a lot of miscommunication. I think it's important that you and the person you're in a relationship with have a good way of communicating with one another. Don't tweet things that are supposed to stay private between the two of you, and don't put each other on blast. Be mature and take the high road.

Online etiquette can be tough to navigate, but I have some real guidelines. The first is never break up with someone over text. It's horrible and cowardly! Do it in person or, as a last resort, verbally over the phone.

Get to know someone in person. Connect with someone in person. Break up with someone in person. Don't hide behind a screen. Anything you say online you should be able to say to whomever you're talking to, be it face-to-face or ear-to-ear.

And speaking of what you say online, think about what you say—or photograph—via text. Many of you may feel pressured to send inappropriate texts and photos to get a boy's attention, but sexting is definitely something to steer clear of. You want a guy to love you for your heart, your mind, and your character, not your body. Sexting teases them and exploits you. How do you know that the guy you're sending these photos and messages to is keeping them private? Even if they do at first, if things don't work out there's a chance whatever you sent can be used against you or shown to others in order to embarrass or shame you.

Be thoughtful about what you share, and you'll be able to avoid this kind of trouble.

BOYS & PARENTS

Earlier in the year, I really liked a boy that my parents did not approve of. It wasn't because they didn't like him as a person, but due to the fact that they set up a few dating rules early on, and this guy broke one. I didn't want to listen to my parents because I thought I knew what was best, but it turned out I should have heeded their advice.

It was the guy I first got in contact with through Snapchat, the one with the adorable dog. He played hockey at the same rink both of my brothers played. I had seen him at the rink for

PLAY IT SAFE ON SOCIAL MEDIA

Follow these tips to stay safe and avoid serious embarrassment (or serious trouble) when socializing online:

Be careful of what you post. Anything you post online is public, and it will be available for the rest of your life. Even if you think you're sending a private message to a close friend, if it's online, it's available to the whole world due to sharing with other friends, screen shots, hacking, and more. Don't send any messages or post anything publicly that you wouldn't say to your parents or read out loud in class.

Be cautious if you plan to meet. Social media is a way to expand your social circle, but there are still precautions you should take when you're meeting someone in person for the first time. Make sure you meet in a brightly lit, public place like a popular restaurant or the mall. Don't go to his house, or invite him to yours. This might be a great time for a group date or one when you bring your best friends along. Be sure to tell people where you're going and with whom.

Check your privacy settings. Keep your posts just for friends unless there's a reason to have followers you don't know personally. You may post sensitive information without even realizing it, like a photo of you and your friends at school that either shows your school name on your uniform or a sign in the background. If someone is really looking for you, they could use your name, your school name, and your hometown to find you. Unclick your location settings.

No one needs to know your exact location. If you do have a public account, like I do, to interact with all of you, check and recheck your pics and text before posting so you aren't unintentionally putting out private information. If you choose to keep your location settings on, be sure to post only *after* you've left that location.

Never share personal information. It may sound obvious, but it's so important, so I'm going to repeat it. Do not share personal information like your home address or phone number, credit card information, or your social security number.

If it feels funny, tell someone. If someone contacts you online, or someone you kind of know asks for personal information or to meet up, tell a parent or adult right away. If the conversation feels off in any way, it's much better to be safe than sorry.

a couple of years, but we are different ages so we never really spoke to each other or formally met. We did follow each other on social media though, which was how I'd seen his puppy post. A few days after we had started talking over Snapchat, I was at the hockey rink watching my brothers and we were formally introduced. We got to talking, and I ended up really liking him after that first meeting. He was so sweet to me and really kind. I hadn't felt that type of connection with a guy before. We began talking nonstop on the phone and through text. He ended up becoming one of my best friends.

After a couple of weeks, I was ready to tell my parents about him. I told my mom and papa all about how much I had begun to like him, and immediately they told me what I did NOT want to hear. They advised me to stop talking to him and not to get invested. Since he was playing at the same rink as my brothers, and only one level above my brother Lev, my parents knew it could cause problems. That's why one of their rules early on was that I couldn't date any hockey players who were in the same leagues as my brothers.

A lot of hockey players would chirp, which is basically trash talk on the ice. Since my brother would sometimes play against

TEXTING TIPS

Start simple. If you're texting, an easy way to start a conversation is by asking a simple question requiring a simple response.

Don't obsess. If you're waiting for a guy to text you back, don't sit by your phone and wait. Get up and occupy yourself. Go for a walk, do your homework, call a friend, watch a movie—literally anything to keep you from staring at your phone.

Know when to call it. You should absolutely respond to him and keep the conversation going if you remain interested, but also recognize when your texting is becoming one-sided.

Be cautious with your tone. When talking over text, it's easy to misinterpret jokes and sarcasm for truth. Make sure the words you're texting have a clear meaning, without an attitude or tone you weren't intending. Using emojis can help clarify the way your words are intended.

the guy that I was interested in, my name would get thrown around by some of the other players. That made my brother very uncomfortable, and for good reason. At one point, my brother even went into the locker room and told the team to leave me out of it and to stop talking about me. For that, I don't know how to ever thank my brother. Although it wasn't the guy I liked saying the rude things, it was our relationship that allowed his teammates to use me against my brother.

My parents knew this would happen, and knew it wasn't right or fair to either of us. But I was only thinking about myself, so I felt like I was being unfairly penalized. Looking back, I wish I had been more conscious of Lev's feelings. It clearly wasn't fair to Lev that he had to hear gross, salacious, and untrue remarks about his sister during games, said just to throw him off or make him mad enough to lash out and get a penalty.

The guy and I ended things a while later, and I'm glad we did. He was not the guy for me. My time with him (in the moment) was great, and I saw nothing wrong, but I should have been more aware of the big picture and listened to my parents.

It can be hard to take your parents' advice on boys (and in this case, my brother as well), but the truth is, they're looking out for your best interests. In this case, my parents didn't want me to become the subject of sports-related trash talking or to become a problem for my brother. That trash talk could have given me a bad reputation (even if it was a lie) and hurt me down the road.

As potentially uncomfortable or intimidating as it may be, it's important to introduce your friends and family to any guy you're interested in dating fairly early on. They usually know you best, and it should be a huge red flag if they have valid concerns or don't get along with him. These meetings can be

PUT THAT JOURNAL TO USE

CRUSHES AND ROMANCE

Love and romance can feel like a rollercoaster ride. You may not want to remember every crush or every detail of past relationships, but writing it down can give you perspective on your own growth and maturity. It will also remind you of the qualities you're looking for in a guy and what pitfalls to avoid. Sometimes people have a "type" of person they gravitate toward, which can be a good or bad thing, depending on what that type is. You may notice patterns in your relationships if you document them, which can help you for future relationships. Best of all, reviewing your love life can bring back memories that will make you giggle. Well, I guess they could make you gag too. Either way, they become stories to tell your kids about some day, and that will open up a whole other world of fun!

nerve-wracking and awkward for sure, but it's worth it to feel confident and comfortable in your relationship. Nothing ruins a relationship faster than hiding and sneaking around, so bring your crush to a casual dinner and feel out the situation.

Dating is great, lots of fun, and even beneficial to help you mature. It allows us to discover what we want out of romantic relationships as we grow up and they in turn become more serious. It's totally okay if you don't connect with someone after a date. Don't put pressure on yourself to couple up or make every possible attraction into a full-fledged relationship. The right person will make himself known to you at the right time. Be patient and enjoy single life in the meantime.

DATING SITUATIONS AND SOLUTIONS

SITUATION: I have a crush on a guy at school. How do I make the first move?

SOLUTION: Go up to him and spark a conversation, or even make some eye contact from across the hall if you're at school. Starting up a conversation is quite easy, and that's the only way you'll ever get to know him. Remember to be yourself and build a friendship first. Sometimes it's even a good idea to have a friend talk to some of his friends, letting them know that you want to get to know him better.

SITUATION: My parents won't let me date, but all my friends are dating. I really want to spend time with a special guy. What do I do?

SOLUTION: I've been through this before. I wasn't allowed to date until I was sixteen, but of course there were guys that I really liked prior to when I was sixteen. It can be frustrating, but you have to respect your parents' rules. I suggest being open and honest with the guy about the no-dating rule. Honesty is the best policy. I'm sure he will understand, as every household has different rules. If you want to spend time together, maybe go out in groups instead of going out one-on-one. If he doesn't understand, then I would say he isn't the guy for you.

SITUATION: I want to go out with a guy who is a few years older. Is that a good idea?

SOLUTION: I think it depends on how much older the guy is. I've always wanted to stay around the same age group as me, because if a guy is much older than I am, we may be on different paths. I want a guy who is of a similar maturity level as me. I think once you get older—in your twenties—it's totally fine to date someone older than you, but always be mindful of where you both are in life. Be clear about what you want, and find out what he wants. Don't ever feel pressured to do anything.

SITUATION: I'm going on my first date and I'm nervous! What should we do on our date? And what should I talk about?

SOLUTION: Suggest daytime activities that are fun and might spark a shared interest, like mini golf, a hike, or a sporting event. Talk about what interests you and get to know each other. Ask lots of questions about his interests, but be careful about bombarding him with questions so it doesn't feel like an interview. Keep the conversations light on a first date.

SITUATION: I'm getting mixed signals from my crush. One day he seems really interested in me, and other days he ignores me. What should I do?

SOLUTION: If you're getting mixed signals, don't stress. If you've showed him you're interested, sit back and let him make the next move. If he doesn't, he may not be as into you as you're hoping, and you should move on. I always tend to overanalyze these things, when in reality they don't need to be overanalyzed! If he is interested, he will make the effort, just like you have.

CHAPTER 6

THE REAL VALUE OF FAMILY

Excuses are for losers.

—BURE FAMILY MOTTO

"Family" isn't defined only by last names or by blood; it's defined by commitment and by love. It means showing up when they need it most. It means having each other's backs. It means choosing to love each other even on those days when you struggle to like each other. It means never giving up on each other.

—DAVE WILLIS

My family is everything to me. I love them with all my heart. I would pick them over anyone, any day.

Some of my favorite memories include fun family activities, like going to hockey games, watching movies, playing board games for hours, cooking, going to museums, traveling the world, and going on vacations.

We enjoy doing everything together. For example, two years ago we had a little family cooking competition. Each kid in our family got to make their own dinner dish for our parents, and they judged who created the best meal. It was our own version of the TV show *Chopped*. Lev made shrimp risotto. Maks made steak sandwiches, and I made a cauliflower soup. It was so fun to cook with my brothers, and adding a competitive aspect to it made it even more of a blast.

I was having such a good time hanging out in the kitchen, messing with my tough opponents, that I ended up forgetting to cook the cauliflower itself. When I went to blend it into the soup, it made my creamy creation taste horrible, which everyone found hilarious.

Every time we do activities together, we end up laughing until we pee our pants . . . no, really, it's happened before.

FOCUS ON FAMILY

Most of us have families who love us and support us no matter what. But if you are someone who comes from a broken home, I pray there are people around you who can fill those roles. This may be your grandparents, aunts or uncles, a school counselor, a coach, or a trusted mentor. Family doesn't limit itself to the people that are related to you by blood. Family is made of the people who love you and will always be there for you.

It's more important than ever to embrace your family as the center of your life and community, because they are the key people who help raise you into the person you will become. Your parents and your extended family create the foundation of who you are and how you live your life, providing the tools you need to become a kind, compassionate, impactful person in this world of ours.

Like I said, family is everything to me. I know they are going to be there with me forever, and will love me unconditionally even when I mess up or don't make the best decisions. They help me and guide me with everything that's going on in my life. Without them, I don't know where I would be.

My faith and my family go hand-in-hand. As a young girl, I was taught about the Bible and about Jesus. The Lord binds my entire family together and provides the foundation we live our lives on. If we didn't have him in our lives, our family dynamic would look utterly different. Our faith brings us much closer together. Almost every morning, before my brothers go to school, my dad will do a devotion with us while we eat breakfast. I love that meaningful time of worship as we start our day. It's an incredible way to start the morning, because I'm able to learn about and praise God with my family.

Parents can be your biggest role models, your biggest advocates, and your biggest source of support throughout your life—if you let them. It's easy to get frustrated with their rules and restrictions when you're caught between the two worlds of adulthood and childhood. That struggle can be frustrating as you continue to grow and change, when maybe your parents can't keep up.

Some days I feel completely independent and ready to take on the world, but other days I want my parents by my side for the unsure moments. It can be hard to accept having an early curfew or having to say no to an invitation to a party, but I know parents make rules because they love me. I remember when I was in eighth and ninth grades, I always wanted to go out with my friends to the movies or the mall, and my parents would *never* let me. If my friends wanted to come over to *my* house, that was allowed. But unless my parents knew my friends' parents well enough, hanging out elsewhere was not something they were fond of.

At the time, I was so upset with them, but looking back, I can see we were just a bunch of kids that were always in and out of trouble. Not serious trouble, mind you, but dumb stuff like getting caught making out in a movie theater and generally being loud and disruptive when we were out and about. With time and trust, my parents became more lenient in letting me hang out with friends, especially when I started consistently making good decisions about who I was with and what we were doing.

My parents and I have argued about a ton of things, from curfew to what kind of clothes are appropriate. I know now it was really smart of my parents to be firm about their rules and stick to them. They taught me to be disciplined and to know the difference between good ideas and not-so-good ideas. It benefitted me back then, and still benefits me now.

Even with tough rules and petty arguments, my parents are extraordinary. I am very close with both my parents and I love spending time with them one-on-one. They're funny, goofy, and cool, but also clear about the expectations they have of me while I'm living under their roof.

GET TO KNOW MY PARENTS

My papa, (*Papa* is what you call a dad in Russian) was born and raised in Russia, and is a very stringent man. He grew up in

TOP 5 WAYS TO GAIN YOUR PARENTS' TRUST

1. If your parents ask you to do something, do it right away and without complaint. No huffing or puffing—trust me, they can hear it. And no eye rolling. They see that too.

2. Be forthcoming with information about your social plans. Share all of the details, including who will be driving, who will be there, and what you're doing.

3. Stay calm if your parents don't allow you to do something or say no to a request. Tears, yelling, and storming off are *not* the ways to show your maturity. It will oftentimes get you in trouble if you do.

4. Admit your mistake if you made one. Did you accidentally run over your mom's rosebush while pulling into the driveway? Go inside immediately and tell her what happened, along with a big, heartfelt apology. She'll appreciate you being honest, especially when you offer to help her plant a new one.

5. Show appreciation for your parents by saying thank you for dinner, helping with the dishes, and even making coffee in the morning before they wake up. It's all about the little things.

Moscow and was raised by his mother and father, but separately because they were divorced. He played hockey as a young boy and moved to the US, where he played in the NHL for ten years. He worked so hard to be able to have the life he has today, and because of that, he wants his children to work hard and earn what we get too. He wants us to go the extra mile, put in the effort, never be lazy, and to respect others.

My papa is someone I could hang out with for hours. We have the best time together, going to lunch, driving around, cooking, and even just doing errands. In many ways, we are exactly alike. However, because we are both extremely stubborn and hardheaded, getting into arguments with each other can seem like World War Three. There have been times when we have gone weeks without saying a word to one another. But in the end, when we are together and both in a good mood, we are two peas in a pod.

My mom, on the other hand, is much different. She is very sweet and kind, and though she's very firm with rules, she has a mother's touch. She knows how to comfort me when I'm having a crummy day and always wants to see me smile. I am super close with my mom, and I really enjoy spending one-on-one time with her.

Since she is always traveling for work, filming TV shows and movies, it can sometimes be difficult to see each other, but we always make it a priority and find the time! Sometimes I visit her on set wherever she is filming, whether it be in New York, Canada, or wherever. One time I visited her while she was filming a movie in Vancouver. It was the perfect girls' weekend, filled with lots of shopping, yummy restaurants, and tons of laugher. We even filmed a YouTube video together while I was there, which you can catch on my channel. I love her and admire her work ethic with everything she does.

I respect my parents' drive to succeed more than anything. They are the hardest-working people I know, and they can achieve anything they put their minds to. Both of my parents went in front of millions and competed in reality television shows: my dad on one called *Battle of the Blades* and my mom on *Dancing with the Stars*. My papa won the competition on his show, and my mom came in third place. They pushed themselves to their limits and came out on top. They are both so accomplished and respected in their fields. It makes me want to do the same to achieve my own goals and make them proud.

They are also two of the most selfless people I know. They are always putting others first. If there is anything that has to do with one of us kids, both of my parents drop what they're doing to support us, even if it means sacrificing something they had planned. There have been times where my mom or papa have had plans to go out to dinner with friends or had a work-related event, but if one of the boys have a hockey event or one of my performances pops up, they are sitting front row.

How well do you know your parents? The better you understand them, the easier it will be to understand why they make the rules that they do. Start by asking them questions about their childhoods, how they got involved in their careers or hobbies, and how they met each other. They'll feel heard and valued just from being asked such questions, and you'll have a better understanding of where they're coming from.

> The better you understand your parents, the easier it will be to understand why they make the rules that they do.

COMMUNICATION & CONFLICT

It's not always easy to be honest and open with your parents. In fact, I used to keep almost *everything* secret from my mom and papa. If I was dealing with a boy or even a tough time at school, I didn't want them to judge me. But I found the more I began to tell my parents about those things and the more open I was, they were able to not only help me more, but they began to trust me more. Don't be scared to talk to your parents. Remember, they were teenagers once too!

Even still, communicating with your parents might not be second nature. Avoid some of the common pitfalls of communicating with your parents by staying calm, taking deep breaths, and listening when you're having a tough conversation. I'll admit, it's easier said than done. I'm the first one to yell and storm off if I'm in any sort of dispute or fight. I really don't like losing arguments, and I always want to come out on top. But over the years I've learned to be slow to speak and quick to listen with my parents. I no longer throw a fit just because something doesn't go my way, and I try to show my parents I can be mature by combatting a change in plans with an understanding attitude.

In 2014, I was so excited when my mom was asked to compete on *Dancing with the Stars*. It was amazing being able to watch her train and compete, and I was so proud of her when she ultimately came in third place. What an accomplishment! I would go to all the Saturday rehearsals, and being there to watch was a special experience for me. During the second week of competition, I got into a silly fight with my parents, and thanks to my bad attitude, I wasn't allowed to go to the performance as my punishment. It really hurt. I had to watch my mom perform from the TV at home, and watch my brothers and Papa cheer her on. My actions not only affected myself, but also my family. I'm sure my mom wanted me to be there to support her, but because I let my frustration get the best of me, I had to pay the price. It was a really tough night for me, and there were a lot of tears, but I definitely learned my lesson.

The Bible teaches us to honor and obey our parents. It's a principle that I've been taught since I can remember. Respect means that you know your boundaries with a person and you are mindful of how you treat someone. I can respect my parents by following their rules, doing what they ask of me, and showing them appreciation. The least I can do is express to my parents that I appreciate everything they do for me and our family.

So even when you're sure you and your parents couldn't be more different, try to remember they have your best interests at heart. They may not fully understand the situation you're facing, and as you begin to branch out on your own and have different experiences, it may seem like they don't understand you at all. But no matter the circumstances, your parents have knowledge and support to offer you. Be open enough to give them the chance to share.

GROWING PAINS

All parents are guilty of occasionally treating their teenagers like young children. Sometimes, we deserve it. Other times, not so much.

There are ways to push boundaries respectfully and to assert yourself if you feel you're not being given enough responsibility or freedom. You can share how you feel without coming off as rude or immature and without overstepping your bounds. There have been times when I felt the need to push back a little and share my opinions, and I've learned the best way to do that is to sit down with my parents and say something like, "I want to talk

GIVE RESPECT, GET RESPECT

Treat others as you want to be treated.

Listen. Even when you have a million things going on in your head, stop and listen to what your parents are saying. Believe me, there is real wisdom and insight if you listen carefully.

Ask questions. If you don't understand what they're telling you or asking you to do, slow down and ask them to clarify.

Be patient. It's easy to feel frustrated and for that to boil over into snapping at your parents. Patience is difficult, I know, but it's one of the most important tools for communication and showing your respect.

Spend time together. Quality time, doing an activity you all love, is the best way to engage and connect with your parents on mutual ground.

to you about these things and tell you how I'm feeling. I want to know if we can make some adjustments, or ask what it would take to change things."

Be prepared for an open dialogue with more questions about the subject. Be prepared to hear what you don't want to hear, but offer up possibilities like setting goals for those changes. Our parents really are on our side. They're just waiting to see our growth in making responsible decisions and mature, respectful conversations are a part of that.

Sometimes your parents are going to say no to your requests. But if you've presented a good case, they might just say yes! Show them how much you appreciate their trust by A) sticking to the new plan, and B) saying thank you.

One of my favorite ways to thank my parents when I was a kid was to make cards for them. I would handcraft cards and write sweet or silly notes in them. The cards would take me a couple hours to make because I had to cut, paint, hot glue, and craft the entire thing by myself, but even though they were time-consuming projects, the cards got my point across—how much I wanted to thank my parents for everything they do.

Find your own way to show your parents you appreciate and

HOW TO NEGOTIATE WITH YOUR PARENTS

Approach the situation like a lawyer. Act professionally, be prepared, envision what the other side is looking for, and be ready to accept the answer you're given.

- **Prove yourself.** Before you start making requests for a later curfew or more independence, make sure you've proven that you're trustworthy and responsible.
- **Do your chores immediately when asked.** Handle your schoolwork and hit those deadlines. Maybe even offer to help out with dinner or a sibling's school project. Show your parents you're ready for a change.
- **Be prepared.** Go into the conversation knowing what you're asking for and why. Consider their potential concerns related to your request, and think about how you might rebut them. You might even want to jot down notes ahead of time so you feel prepared.

Take it seriously. Make the conversation feel more formal than a casual chat on your way out the door. Sit down at the dining room table with good posture, eye contact, and no distractions. Extra points if you start by thanking them for their time.

Stay calm. Your parents are willing to hear you out, so calmly and clearly make your case. If the conversation isn't going your way, it might be second nature to dissolve into tears, pout or whine, or act in other ways that undermine your point. Maybe the answer is no today, but it doesn't mean it will stay no. If you handle yourself well, your parents may reconsider.

Be ready to negotiate. You may not get an immediate yes to your request, but rather a counteroffer. Let's say you're asking for a midnight curfew, and your parents come back with ten pm. Well, it's a starting point. Thank them for their consideration and ask if eleven pm might work. Or, use continued responsibility over time to get you what you want in a few months. If the ten o'clock curfew goes well and you're on time every night for the next month, perhaps they'll consider 10:30 after that.

Be ready for a no. Despite your best efforts to make a compelling case and hold a mature conversation, you need to be prepared that the answer may still be no. Not getting what you want is a part of life, and even if you go into a conversation ready for the discussion and with a good attitude, there is still a chance you won't succeed. It's still important to show maturity by maintaining a respectful attitude toward the decision. It sets you up for success in the future.

love them. Write them a letter or a poem. Cook them a special dinner (and be sure to clean up after). Do an activity they love to do and you normally avoid, like going to the hardware store with your dad or gardening with your mom. Other ways are super simple: a hug and a heartfelt "thank you" or "I love you" will go a long way. It's the little things that mean the most!

BROTHERLY LOVE

I grew up with two younger brothers and no other girls in the house. Lev is eighteen months younger, and Maksim is three and a half years younger. When I was young, having two brothers was fun—we'd go on bike rides, build forts, make tree houses, go on scavenger hunts, and wrestle. But when I hit middle school and the beginning of high school, things definitely changed. They no longer wanted to hang out with me all the time; they wanted to do their own thing. I started feeling like the odd man out.

Lev and I are pretty close in age, but because I'm older, a lot of the things I was allowed to do, he wasn't. If he wasn't able to have the same privileges as I did, he would get upset and we'd end up fighting. Those arguments caused tension in my family, and Lev and I ended up feeling resentful toward one another. Eventually, we were able to get past those feelings, but that competition was hard to overcome.

Competition wasn't the only tough part about having two brothers. Siblings often tease each other, and my brothers did it non-stop. They'd tease me about everything from boys, my dance moves, them being better than me, to other silly little things. Other topics and jabs could be hurtful though, like when they'd make comments about my acne. They weren't

PARENTS: SITUATIONS AND SOLUTIONS

SITUATION: I've broken my parents' trust. How can I rebuild our relationship?

SOLUTION: I know what you're feeling: the remorse, the guilt, the heartbreak over disappointing your parents and yourself. I've broken my parents' trust many times in my life, and I still do sometimes. You can't rebuild that trust all at once, but you can over time. Show them you're trustworthy by obeying what they ask each day and going above and beyond. Do the dishes without being asked. Clean up the house and fluff the pillows. Pick up your room. Ask if either of your parents needs help with anything. Show them that you *want* to gain their trust back. If your parents see the drive inside of you and see the effort you are putting in, they will recognize the changes you've made.

SITUATION: I'm jealous of my sister, because everything seems to come easily to her. She's beautiful and smart and very popular. How can I get past this?

SOLUTION: I can relate to this with my younger brother Lev. He is incredibly smart and one of the most athletic kids I know. He's also handsome and makes friends super easily. I used to compare myself to him and felt like I never stacked up. Sometimes I would lash out at home and say hurtful things. With your sister, don't be jealous; instead, be happy that she's successful and well-liked, and appreciate her accomplishments. I'm sure there are plenty of things that you are talented at that she isn't. Everyone thinks the grass is greener on the other side, but sometimes we forget to look at how green our side is too!

SITUATION: My brother is making bad choices—lying to our parents and sneaking out at night. I don't want to tell my parents and get him in trouble, but I'm worried about him. What should I do?

SOLUTION: I was in a similar situation during my senior year of high school with my brother. Growing up, I was always the one being tattled on, but I realized I was the one who needed to help set him straight this time. I saw that he was up to no good, so I told him that he should stop fooling around and make better choices moving forward. In the end, my parents ended up finding out their own way, without me spilling the beans. It all ended up working out, but if a situation gets dangerous or out of hand, tell your parents and don't worry about tattling. Your brother's well-being is the number one priority.

SITUATION: My parents don't approve of my boyfriend because he doesn't share the same beliefs as we do. I really like him, and I don't want to stop seeing him. What should I do?

SOLUTION: It's important to get to know and be friends with people of all different beliefs. However, if your beliefs are important to you, take what your parents are saying into serious consideration. You shouldn't compromise your beliefs for any one person (including a boy). Be open and honest, and discuss this with him. It may be super frustrating and heartbreaking, but until you're older and decide how important your religion is to you, I would make a decision that honors your family.

SITUATION: My parents are very religious, and I don't agree with their beliefs. How can I tell them this without hurting their feelings?

SOLUTION: If you don't believe in the religion that your parents do, don't be afraid to have conversations with them about it. Religious beliefs are important. You don't have to undermine their teaching or disrespect what they believe in, but tell them what you're thinking. Most of all, allow yourself to explore the reasons why you feel differently. If their beliefs aren't for you, what is? Do research and get educated. Ask your parents and religious teachers questions and find some answers.

trying to hurt me, but their words shot down my self-esteem very quickly.

Thankfully, my relationships with my brothers have changed over the years. The last couple of months of my senior year, Lev and I became much closer and grew to understand that we would always have each other's back. We both knew that if we worked together, we could do what we wanted without fighting and arguing. Finding compromises and learning to do things together definitely helped. Now he is one of my best friends. Yes, we still fight and bicker and tease each other, but at the end of the day, he supports me and I support him. It's a win-win when we are both on the same page.

I've learned firsthand how important it is to have close relationships with your siblings. You grow up in the same household, with the same parents, many of the same memories and experiences, and the same values. It's like having a built-in friend who knows you better than almost anyone. I'm glad I'm close with my brothers—even when they drive me crazy. I hope that as we grow into adults, our relationships continue to grow and get even stronger. It's not always easy for us to see eye-to-eye, but the better we get to know each other and the more we respect one another, the easier it gets to be friends *and* siblings.

As much as I love my brothers, having them respect my

LET'S ALL GET ALONG

Find a common activity. Choose just one thing that you and your brother or sister enjoy, and do it together regularly. The camaraderie from sharing an activity will help smooth over bickering around the house.

Take a break. Don't spend all your time together. Go out with your friends, or spend some time alone in your room. It will help you appreciate the fun you do have together with your siblings.

Embrace traditions. From big holiday celebrations to something as simple as pancake Sundays, it's cool to enjoy time with your family. Traditions also help you build special moments you'll look back on later.

Work together. Find a common goal and tackle it together. You'll be more efficient in the task at hand, and you may learn to appreciate something new about one another.

See things from their perspective. Talk to them the way you want to be talked to—with respect, love, kindness, and helpfulness.

privacy is essential to our getting along. For me, having time alone so I can gather my thoughts and be in my own space is extremely valuable.

If you are able to have your own room in your house, then use your space to your advantage! Express your individuality by decorating it to your taste, and organize it so you can spend time doing the things you want to do there. It's your oasis within the house, a place to do your own thing, unwind, and reflect. I live in a super busy household, but when I get those spare moments when I can just be by myself, I take advantage of the opportunity!

That privacy and time alone can help you grow closer with your family. You're more likely to appreciate the craziness of

TIP **Change your role.** If you feel like you're in a rut with your family—acting and reacting in the same negative, ineffective ways—you have the power to change it. Use the exercises from chapter 1 to remind yourself who you are, and to evaluate if you're acting authentically. Take the time to observe your reactions and work on slowly making changes. For example, if your little brother barges into your room without knocking, and you always shout at him to stop and then slam the door, perhaps an alternative reaction is needed. For example, talk to your parents calmly about a lock or holding "open door" times when your brother is welcome to come in, so he's not tempted to come in when not invited. You can outsmart your emotional reactions!

daily life when you've had time to yourself. You can see your family through fresh eyes.

At the end of the day, no matter how nuts your brother or sister or mom or dad seems, you know you'll love them anyway. That's the best part of being a family—the people who love you are there for you when you need them most. So instead of focusing on all the ways you're different from each other, look for the silly, funny, and caring moments that bring you closer together.

The relationships between family members and the atmosphere of your home is so important to your daily life, the health and well-being of your family, and in living according to your faith. Treat your family with generosity and kindness, and that's the kind of household—and world—you'll live in. All of this craziness and love adds to who you are.

CHAPTER 7

REAL HEALTH

*Do you not know that your bodies are
temples of the Holy Spirit, who is in you,
whom you have received from God? You are
not your own; you were bought at a price.
Therefore honor God with your bodies.*

—1 CORINTHIANS 6:19-20

Showing love to our bodies is important. This means making smart food choices, exercising regularly, and getting enough rest (both mentally and physically) so that our bodies are in the best health they can be. I always feel a thousand times better when I'm eating clean foods and drinking lots of water . . . even though I may or may not have a love affair with ice cream and milkshakes. (Everything is good in moderation, right?) I do my best to balance my sweet-tooth with a lot of healthy fruits and vegetables, and lean proteins like fish or grilled chicken. See? Balance!

Similarly, exercising is one of the best ways I take care of myself, relieve stress, and stay fit. I try to work out every day, but it doesn't always happen, and that's okay. Some days I don't feel like doing a strenuous workout, but I'll take a walk, go for a swim, play tennis with my papa, or go to a dance class—hip-hop classes are my favorite—just to get moving. You might consider joining a sport, trying yoga, or even looking up some quick-and-easy-workout videos online. Simply moving around for at least fifteen to thirty minutes a day can make a huge difference.

Our bodies are amazing, and it's our job to take care of them. It's okay if you're not a gym girl or a strict vegetarian—there are tons of other ways to keep our bodies healthy and fit. And the most important step toward that goal is understanding the beauty of your own body, even if you don't look anything like the girl on the cover of this month's *Vogue*. Because let's be real . . . almost no one does.

BODY IMAGE

Young women are constantly being sent mixed messages about what a "perfect" body truly looks like. Fashion and beauty magazines, movies, television commercials, and social media posts continue to feature unattainably thin, airbrushed, gorgeous models who would make even the most beautiful girls feel inadequate. And at the same time, these companies are trying to promote the idea of loving yourself at any size . . . even if

> Our bodies are amazing, and it's our job to take care of them.

that's not what they're showing in their ads. It's a confusing time, though we're starting to move in the right direction by opening up the conversation and calling out the industry, especially with the help of women like Alicia Keys, Kelly Clarkson, and Zendaya. But body image issues aren't a thing of the past yet, and with the influence of social media and the constant barrage of flawless photos, the pressure to be thin, beautiful, and perfect can really take a toll on many of us.

The pressures are out there to change the way you look in order to get attention from others. In so many parts of our lives, we're judged by our appearance, and we all want to impress our friends, our bosses, and our crushes. So it's understandable to start thinking, *Should I dye my hair? Should I lose weight? Should I change my lips?* Those are all things that I hear girls say on a daily basis.

Many people living in LA are in the entertainment industry and have these crazy-beautiful model bodies: tall, slender, "perfect" figures. There are so many models, actors, musicians, and dancers who are expected to look a certain way. I have compared myself to them plenty of times. But that's not me. I'm 5'4" and I have curves . . . but that doesn't mean I'm not beautiful. I'm shaped completely differently than my best friend . . . but that doesn't mean she's more or less beautiful than me. So instead of dwelling on what I don't like, I've learned to appreciate the features that make me special. There is no other Natasha Bure. I am unique, and so are you. The bottom line is, everyone is made to be different, and we should celebrate that.

Don't let social media, movies, advertisements, and all the images of perfect bodies fog your perception of who you are and how you feel about yourself and your body. Every person on earth is fearfully and wonderfully made by God, and we are all built differently. If you have a fuller figure or are extra petite, own it. Different skin color, hair texture, being short or tall—whatever it may be, rock what God gave you. Each of us is beautiful in our own way.

And most of all, strive to be your healthiest self.

INSIDE OUT

Feeling good about yourself and being comfortable in your body starts with what's inside. There are many factors that play into how we see and feel about ourselves, but ultimately we decide what those are. No one has the power to make you feel ugly or beautiful unless you give it to them. Even before you begin to focus on eating right and fitness, focus on the person you want to become. Find friends that strengthen you and make you happy when you are around them. Pick activities, sports, or hobbies that inspire you to be your best self. Working on who you are inside is way more important than working on who you are on the outside. And you know what? The healthier and happier your heart and mind are, the healthier and happier your body will be.

So don't worry about other people's idea of what "perfection" is. In reality, perfect is not something that exists, except when it comes to Jesus Christ. God made you just the way he wanted to . . . though that doesn't mean you can sit around and be lazy with the body he gave you. Care for your beautiful body and give yourself the attention, love, and respect you deserve.

My parents are an inspiration to me when it comes to taking great care of my body. They always stress how important it is to take care of myself not only spiritually and mentally but also physically. In fact, my mom has completely transformed her outlook on food and her body. She even wrote about it in her book *Reshaping It All*. And because my papa is a professional athlete and Olympian, I have no excuse not to know a thing or two about health and fitness.

FITNESS

Healthy living doesn't have to be hard. In fact, it should be fun to engage in activities and build habits that make you feel good. Exercise, in particular, is not only good for your body, it makes you so much happier. The benefits of exercise are pretty staggering. I

LEARN TO LOVE YOUR BODY

Move your body. It's hard to feel down on yourself when you're engaged in an activity you love and your body begins releasing those powerful, natural endorphins. So go for a jog, take your favorite spin class, or work out at home using a fitness app as your guide.

Focus on the positives. It's easy to focus on what you don't like about yourself, but it's important to focus on what you love. Stand in front of the mirror and appreciate the features you're proudest of—your strong, athletic legs; your almond-shaped eyes; your smile; and so forth. Practice positive self-talk, and soon it will become a habit. If you're just having one of those days and can't muster up the positivity to list all of your beautiful attributes, then have your go-to, feel-good items ready as backup. The shiny lip gloss that makes you look fierce, your super flattering jeans, or the top that just makes you feel cool. When I'm having a crummy day, I'll put on makeup and my favorite outfit just to boost my confidence. I blast my favorite music and jam out while getting ready, even if I don't have anywhere to go. It's the little things that can boost your confidence, and confidence is one of the most attractive things in a person. Once you find your groove, you'll get through the day in relatively good spirits, and the negativity will pass.

Don't let a number or a size dictate how you feel. Take good care of your body by focusing on being heart healthy. We all have different shapes, builds, and proportions, so numbers and sizes can be somewhat irrelevant. Check with your doctor to make sure you're within a healthy range for your body type. If you are, great! If you aren't, create a plan with your doctor or parents so that you can start to make the necessary adjustments. And remember, God's love for you will never change no matter how much your body changes. He will always love you no matter what size or weight you are.

Run your own race. Don't compare yourself to your favorite actress or celeb, or even your best friend. Set goals that are right for you, enjoy the process of working hard to improve, and celebrate your successes. More often than not, there's someone admiring you too—whether it's because of your eyes, your hair type, or your ability to be honest or genuine—even if they never say it out loud.

can't remember a time where I came out of an exercise class and didn't feel more awake and have a more positive spirit.

My workout schedule is all over the place depending on the day and my other activities, and I'll admit I prefer "fun" exercise the most. Running, for example, is a great workout, but I find it boring and monotonous. I would much rather get my cardio in other ways, like the elliptical machine, dance classes, or taking cardio kickboxing classes. Those are all great ways to get your heart rate up, and because I actually enjoy doing them, I'm more likely to stay committed and continue exercising.

When I'm on top of my workout routine, I try to do about thirty to forty-five minutes of cardio and then, depending on the day, I will do a core workout circuit that focuses on different muscles in my body. There are different exercises that strengthen and tone my abs, legs, arms, butt, and other key muscles. If I am ever with my papa or my mom's trainer, Kira Stokes—which is a big treat!—they help me do exercises I normally wouldn't do on my own. I love working out with someone who is tough and pushes me to get me into better shape.

I know that not everyone has access to or can afford a trainer, fitness classes, or a gym membership. The good news is working out doesn't have to cost a thing. There are tons of activities that are free and that you can do anywhere, whether you live near the warm, sunny beach, in the high mountains, or in a snow-filled city. And free fitness trainers are always just an app or Google search away. So get out and get moving!

When getting active, you can always bring a buddy too. Having a partner increases your accountability, and it's just more fun to sweat with a friend. Instead of meeting up at a coffee shop to sit and talk, go for a walk together, take a bike ride, or head to the gym.

These are easy ways to stay active and spend quality time with your family or friends. Just remember to put in the physical effort and not get too distracted while gabbing away. (It happens to all of us!)

MORE THAN JUST EXERCISE

Lots of girls start exercising because they want to lose weight and tone up, which, of course, regular workouts can help you do. But there are a lot of other reasons to get moving besides fitting into your skinny jeans. Here are just some of the incredible benefits of working out:

- Joining sports teams at school or even a recreational league in your area can help you meet new friends.
- Going on long walks or hikes can help you explore your neighborhood or a nearby park and give you some much-needed time in nature to relax and de-stress.
- Learning a new skill, like how to ski or dance, may show you a new passion you didn't know you had.
- When you exercise, your body releases feel-good hormones that help reduce stress and anxiety and put you in a good mood for the rest of the day.
- Building muscle helps you in your daily routine as you lift your shopping bags or your little brother, and it helps you maintain good posture.
- In the long run, regular exercise may even reduce your risk of serious illnesses like heart disease or high blood pressure. You're probably not thinking about that now, but you should know that the benefits are huge.

MY GO-TO WORKOUT

I love to do cardio and then round out my workout with a few toning exercises. Below is a list of my favorite exercises, which are perfect to do at home or in the gym. You can alternate exercises to focus on different areas on different days, or swap in your favorites.

1. **Cardio.** Find a way to do cardio, whether it's running, swimming, the elliptical machine, a dance class, biking— whatever you decide. Keep up a good heart rate for about thirty minutes or so to reap the maximum benefits. If you're not quite up to that yet, try starting out with fifteen or twenty minutes and work your way up. The point is to move and sweat a little. And the more you work out, the better you'll get and the more you'll enjoy it!

2. **Circuit training.** Here is a list that I usually follow. Do three sets of ten reps each. I usually take a one-minute break between each set. I do all three sets of an exercise before moving on to the next.

   □ Ten sit-ups
   □ Ten pushups
   □ Ten leg step ups (per leg)
   □ Thirty seconds of Russian Twists
   □ Twenty squats
   □ Ten triceps pushups
   □ Thirty seconds of scissor kicks
   □ Twenty booty blasters (per leg)
   □ Thirty seconds of jump lunges
   □ Forty-five second core plank

HEALTHY EATING

We all know its super important to eat well—a healthy, balanced diet with lots of fruits, vegetables, whole grains, and lean proteins. But when we're juggling school, homework, social activities, chores, and work, it can be hard to take the time to eat well. It's so easy to fill up on vending machine snacks, fast food, and convenient but unhealthy foods in the school cafeteria. And who doesn't socialize at Starbucks with a caramel Frappuccino, extra whipped cream? All of it tastes good, but too much indulging can come at the price of our health.

Things can get complicated as you begin to assert your preferences and desire for healthy eating while still living with your parents, who are probably in charge of the nightly menu. One of the benefits of living in a household with three male athletes is that there is always healthy food for me to eat because they want to stay in shape as well. But that may not be the case for you, so as you learn more about good nutrition and what your body needs, you'll need to make polite suggestions to your mom or dad, or learn how to cook a healthy substitution for yourself. For example, when grocery shopping, pick up some healthy veggies

TIP When you know you have a busy day ahead, pack a few healthy snacks that are easy to carry and will keep you going. Try a protein bar, cut-up veggies with hummus, yogurt and some nuts, or even half a sandwich on whole-grain bread. These are all much better alternatives to whatever you find in a vending machine or drive-thru!

MY CAFETERIA DOS AND DON'TS

As you navigate the cafeteria at school every day, there are so many unhealthy, fattening, and chemical-filled—yet tempting—choices. Try my tips to steer clear of decisions you'll regret, or try bringing your lunch from home so you know exactly what you're eating. You can bring leftovers from last night's healthy dinner, or classic turkey or tuna sandwiches or salads. Bringing your lunch puts you in control and takes you out of the lunch line, where all kinds of snacks and treats might tempt you.

Do choose a salad or hit the salad bar. Just go easy on dense, high-calorie toppings like cheeses and creamy salad dressing.

Don't get dessert with your meal. If you get it, you'll definitely eat it. Wait until you finish eating to decide if you really want that dessert. If you do, eat a small portion.

Do add a piece of fruit to your meal. It'll give you a sweet pick-me-up that can replace a dessert.

Don't go for anything fried, covered in pepperoni, dripping in oil, or with orange cheese layered on top. Carb-loading like that can lead to an energy crash later in the day.

Do eat a hearty, healthy breakfast at home in the morning so you're not starving by lunchtime and tempted to grab the easiest option to satisfy your hunger.

Don't skip meals entirely. Not only does this *not* help you lose weight, you'll also feel more tired and weak, and lose your stamina during school. It's better to eat smaller meals several times a day or roughly every three hours.

that you can keep in the fridge. I love making veggie stir-fry—it's easy and super healthy!

It can be even harder to make healthy choices when you're out with your friends or getting lunch in the school cafeteria. The best strategy is to approach each meal with a plan. For instance, during high school, I packed lots of cut-up fruit and veggies. I would have my mom pick up grapes, apples, carrots, celery, and cucumbers. I'd slice them up the night before or morning of and put them in baggies for my lunch. If you want something to dip them in, pack a very small container filled with peanut butter or your favorite salad dressing or hummus. This is an easy way to add more flavor to your snacks. But remember, don't eat too much of the dressing or peanut butter. Even though they are good-for-you fats, any fats in excess aren't good for you.

My particular philosophy on food is to eat everything in moderation. I am someone who loves bread, pasta, and ice cream, but if I eat it too much and too often, I end up feeling sluggish and unhealthy. Instead of cutting these from my diet completely, I just eat them in smaller portions and make sure the rest of my diet is full of healthy choices.

I love to eat fish, fruits, vegetables, grains, and drink lots of water. I know these are the foods that give my body the energy it needs, and I end up feeling good when I eat them consistently. I like keeping tomatoes, cucumbers, and avocados in my fridge. I chop them all up, add a little olive oil, and I have a yummy little salad! Or if I'm looking for a protein-packed snack, I'll make a simple chicken salad. I cut one chicken breast into smaller, bite-sized pieces and sauté it in a pan with a little bit of olive oil and salt and pepper. Once the chicken is cooked through, I add it to a bed of mixed greens and then throw in any other toppings I'm in the mood for. My favorites are cherry tomatoes and chopped bell peppers.

For snacks, I keep oranges and apples in my fridge, and

A TYPICAL DAY OF MEALS

Breakfast: Eggs (over easy) or whatever delicious meal my dad makes. Sometimes he makes breakfast sandwiches or pancakes; it all depends on the day. We usually have bagels in our house that are an easy option for me. Always yummy!

Lunch: I really love fish, so I will usually have something like grilled salmon or sushi. When I order sushi, I'm careful to avoid rolls that have fried fish or shrimp inside, and instead go for the fresh salmon, albacore tuna, yellowtail, and halibut. Those are all yummy and healthy for you too! Salads and sandwiches are great options too. When I order a salad, I ask for the dressing on the side so I can control how much I use.

Dinner: Dinner usually consists of a salad and then some sort of meat like chicken or fish, or maybe even soup. My dad is a pretty incredible chef, so he always makes something delicious and healthy.

Snack: Some of the snacks I love include avocado toast, healthy smoothies, chopped-up veggies, frozen grapes (which I mentioned earlier in the chapter—trust me, you'll die when you try them), and healthy trail mixes. Don't get me wrong—I'm a sucker for junk food, especially Goldfish crackers, BBQ chips, and cookies. But when I'm focusing on eating clean and living a healthy lifestyle, those are rare treats.

> **TIP** My favorite, easy smoothies have just a few in-gredients and are a refreshing snack. I take any type of frozen fruit that I have, like strawberries, blue-berries, or mangos, then add one banana, some ice, and finally orange juice or almond milk. Blend it all up, and there you go.

bananas out on the counter. Try frozen grapes too! After a couple of hours in the freezer, they taste like mini Popsicle bites. They are so fun to eat while watching a movie. Snack on something like that instead of buttered popcorn or candy.

Of course, I do have times when I make poor eating deci-sions, especially when I'm stressed, bored, or during "that time of the month." Sometimes all I want to do is sit in bed and eat a pint of ice cream. Sometimes stress gets to me and I give in to my cravings—something I particularly did during finals in high school. I get super stressed and just come home and eat. A few hours later, I'll notice my stomach is bloated and I just feel gross. So I do my best not to let my stress dictate what I eat.

I've also never taken on a diet to drop weight quickly, but when I do want to lose a few pounds and feel better, I usually stay away from carbs, high-sugar content, and dairy. Every time I cut those out of my diet, I feel so much better and look much slimmer. Diets can wreak havoc on your body, especially when you're young, so the best way to maintain a healthy weight is to eat properly and avoid the foods that lead to bloating and weight gain.

Learning to make healthier choices about what you put in your body isn't as difficult as it seems. Even with all of the influ-ences from our friends and the social cues that lead us to eat and drink more than we intend, you control everything you put in your body. Start one meal and one decision at a time, and soon, through regularly making good choices, you'll begin to establish lasting healthy habits.

Be conscious of how much you're eating! Eating slowly is one of the best things you can do to stop yourself from eating too much. When you eat quickly, your body can't register how much it's taking in, and you'll end up eating a lot more before you feel full. If you eat slowly and really chew your food, your body can process the amount and give you the "full" signal a lot sooner and more accurately.

So often, we end up eating when we're not hungry. In reality, we might be tired, bored, stressed, or even just thirsty. Before you give in to your midafternoon snack attack, try to appease your hunger with something else. If you think you're bored, find an activity to do. Instead of immediately heading for a bag of potato chips, drink a big glass of water. Take a walk around the block to relieve stress. Food should never consume your life, and you should only consume what is right for you.

TIP Be careful what you drink! Read the labels of any beverage you drink besides plain water. You may think you're making a healthy choice, but you might be surprised how many servings and grams of sugar per serving are in your favorite iced tea, juice, or sports drink. Who wants to waste calories on a drink? It's best to stick with water and flavored seltzer as your go-to drinks, which are also calorie- and chemical-free.

WELL-ROUNDED HEALTH

There are many factors that play into your overall health, and it's not just about dieting and staying active. You should take pride in your appearance and your health, and spend just a little time and energy to make sure you're taking care of yourself. There's nothing more beautiful than a bright-eyed, energetic girl with glowing skin (thanks to hydration, diet, and sleep), and there is a lot more to developing and maintaining overall health than just diet and exercise.

MENTAL HEALTH

Mental health is just as important as physical health. I have struggled at times with not being mentally positive. I would get super down on myself over a bad grade, an argument with my parents, or a lost game. And the more emotional I got, the less I would be motivated to do something about it.

I dealt with a lot of negativity when it came to playing sports. Any time I would play in a tennis match and be down in score, negative and unhealthy thoughts like *You're already a loser, You're a horrible player,* and *You should just quit now* came to mind. These thoughts never helped me, and it took me a long time to learn how to tune those thoughts out. My parents spent a lot of time talking to me about things I was going through, and they prayed and helped me look to the Bible for strength. I'm thankful for that, now more than ever. But sometimes we, as teens, need someone outside of our parents to help us work out our problems. And if feel you are at that point, there are a few different ways to get the extra help you need.

Different options work better for different people, and as a result there are a lot of ways to work through the things we wrestle with. You can talk to a trusted friend or someone at school or church you feel comfortable with and who will keep your conversation confidential. It's important to open up and express all of the worries, anger, or heartbreak you're struggling with, and it helps to be able to talk to someone who is impartial. If some of the feelings you want to sort out are about your parents or family, then it can be difficult to talk to your mom openly and honestly. Find someone you trust, who you know will give you good and sound advice, but who isn't involved in whatever you're dealing with.

For me, one thing that really helped when I was struggling emotionally was therapy—deeper, more formal guidance. I've always struggled with internal, built-up anger. It's probably been my biggest weakness. I would oftentimes react irrationally because it was so hard to properly convey my emotions. I would act out and throw unnecessary fits, or I'd hide in my closet, cry, and not say a word to anyone as to why. Trying to explain to my parents what I was feeling in a more productive way was very difficult for me. They are talkers, and would always try to get me to express my feelings before I'd hit explosion level. But I felt myself shutting down every time they attempted to pull my thoughts out. One day, my parents suggested it might be helpful to talk to a professional about how to deal with my emotions.

I started therapy at the end of my freshman year of high school. At first, I was embarrassed to go. I didn't want people to think something was "wrong" with me, so I only told a couple of my close friends. I went to therapy on and off for about three years, and if I can tell you one thing, it's that *it helps*! I talked to my therapist about everything I was feeling and dealing with.

During my sessions, I got things off my chest that I usually couldn't, and it felt safe. I felt more open and more myself.

I ended up finding out later that a lot of my friends went or still go to therapy. Everyone has different reasons . . . and whatever they are, it's okay. Who wouldn't want to talk about their feelings and get an emotional release? I know I do! That's why I really like to stress the importance of good mental health. No matter what method works best for you, keeping your mind sound is key to living a joyful and peaceful life.

STRESS

It's normal to have stress, and almost anything can cause it—from school, grades and homework, to drama or uncertainty with friends, to the pressures you put on yourself to get into the right college or look a certain way. But you should try to remember that stress can have a very negative impact on you physically and emotionally.

Stress affects so many things in your life! It can affect how you act toward others, your mood, and even your skin. I know that I get horrible breakouts anytime I get stressed out. Other common signs that stress is starting to take its toll can be your heart beating faster, knots in your stomach, muscle tightness, or a general feeling of anxiety.

I would get very stressed whenever I would leave school assignments to the last minute. I would get all worked up even though it was my fault for leaving it to the last minute. When I'm faced with stress now, I always have to take a step back, take a deep breath, recite Scripture, and think positively. What can I do to fix this situation? What should I have done to prevent this? Make sure you are keeping your thoughts filled with positive reinforcements while you're taking a step back.

COPING WITH STRESS

1. **Exercise.** Get outside and go for a run or walk. Taking some time to clear your head, breathe deeply, and enjoy the sunshine will help.

2. **Take a break.** Don't let the stress take over your life. Grab a friend and laugh over fro-yo, listen to your favorite music, take a long shower or bath, or even go to the movies. Sometimes getting out of a negative headspace can help give you perspective.

3. **Talk it out.** Find a trusted friend, teacher, or parent to really talk through what's stressing you out and what you can do to fix it.

4. **Pray.** Prayer is so important. Pray that God will put you at ease toward the tough situation and help you through it.

5. **Focus on solutions.** It can be easy to get caught up in the emotional reaction to stress. But with a clear head, try to focus that energy on possible solutions instead. Create a list of the steps you can take to make up for the bad grade on the midterm or mend your friendship. Breaking any problem down into smaller pieces makes it feel more manageable.

SLEEP

According to the National Sleep Foundation teens need about eight to ten hours of sleep each night to function at their best. If you miss out on sleep—and we all deal with too much homework, late-night events, or even getting stuck in a Netflix rabbit hole—you'll notice you're slower to process information the next day, irritable, and maybe even more likely to get sick.

The benefits of a good night's sleep include everything from helping your memory before a big test to improving your skin to helping you win tomorrow's soccer game. Plus, you'll save a ton of money on lattes if you're making sure you're a bit more rested.

Set yourself up for a good night sleep by wearing comfortable, breathable pajamas and making your room cool and dark. I can pretty much sleep anywhere, but when I'm home, I love sleeping in my bed with all the lights out and an air diffuser on. An air diffuser is a little machine that diffuses calming, scented oils into the air (I love using peppermint, lavender, or thieves). I also turn my phone off when I sleep. I don't want to be woken up by it at all.

A good sleep schedule is just as important as a nice, cozy bed. Anytime I would stay up too late to cram for an exam or finish an assignment, I would always goof up or do something wrong! While it can be tempting to stay out late and sleep until noon—which usually means you'll wake up feeling groggy and still exhausted—you will feel way more awake and motivated if you stick to a routine. I try to get to bed by ten o'clock on weeknights and wake up around seven in the morning for those full eight to ten hours.

Rest—for both your mind and your body—is a key element to your overall health. When you combine eating well, exercising regularly, and getting plenty of sleep, you'll be amazed at the difference in your life. You'll have more energy, feel better, and even *look* better simply by taking care of the body God gave you.

It's important to establish healthy habits when you're young and to learn to love yourself and your body, just the way you are. Healthy habits and a baseline of fitness are things that will benefit your whole life. Try to develop good habits now that will last forever.

CHAPTER 8

REAL BEAUTY

Your beauty should not come from outward adornment, such as elaborate hairstyles and the wearing of gold jewelry or fine clothes. Rather, it should be that of your inner self, the unfading beauty of a gentle and quiet spirit, which is of great worth in God's sight.

—1 PETER 3:3–4

I grew up a tomboy, always playing with my younger brothers and never having time for girly clothes or makeup, unless mud and dirt count. Any picture of me before the age of ten featured raggedy old T-shirts, athletic shorts, and tennis shoes. I always wanted to be in something comfortable so I could run around and be active—climbing trees to make a tree house, splashing in mud puddles, or playing on the basketball and volleyball courts. I never let my mom brush my hair either, which made for *beautiful* photographs. (Sorry, Mom!) I don't think I even started to enjoy wearing dresses until I was in sixth grade.

My interest in beauty came when I entered my freshman year of high school. My mom and I had a lot of our conversations in her bathroom in the mornings, but really, I was watching her put on her makeup and blow-dry her hair. She had a lot of makeup on her counter, in baskets and in organized containers in her drawer, and I found myself always going in there to play around with it. Soon, she started giving me any makeup that she didn't use or want anymore. Secretly, I think she was happy I was finally taking an interest in it.

As I got older, I loved watching YouTube tutorials to learn how to create cool looks and what products to buy. Times of boredom at home turned into creating looks for fun. It didn't matter that I wasn't going anywhere; I was learning how to become an artist for when I did. I wanted to know how to create a natural look that would enhance my features for everyday, as well as something more dramatic for when I got dressed up. I started reading fashion and beauty magazines like *People StyleWatch*, *Allure*, *InStyle*, and *Lucky* to get inspiration.

One of my biggest early inspirations was watching my mom while she was filming the ABC Family show *Make It or Break It*. I would visit her on set and spend a lot of time in hair and makeup, observing the makeup artists as they made up my mom. I became super interested in all of the products and techniques, asking questions about which tools they liked and how they achieved a certain look. Sometimes the makeup artists or hair stylists would have me sit in the chair and play around with makeup. One time I was on set, the hairdresser gave me a pink extension. I felt like the coolest girl in the world.

I didn't start out caring much about my looks, and even though I now enjoy cute clothes and makeup, I'm glad I grew up as a tomboy. For so many years, I put having fun and being myself *way* ahead of thinking about outward appearances. So now, even though I struggle with self-esteem issues from time to time, I try to remember my younger self laughing and running wild, not caring if my hair was a mess or my clothes were in fashion. That's the real me, no matter how I look or what I wear.

REAL BEAUTY

Beauty is so much more than your body type, your haircut, and your makeup prowess. You may have heard the lines from the old Jim Carey movie *Liar Liar*, when his son says to him, "My teacher tells me real beauty's on the inside." And Jim Carey's character responds, "No, that's just something ugly people say." Even though it's meant to be funny, I know some people really do feel that saying beauty is on the inside is a consolation line. Well, I'm here to tell you that it's not. The majority of true beauty

> Beauty is about your heart, your compassion for others, and your character.

does come from within. Beauty is about your heart, your compassion for others, and your character. It's also about embracing who God made you to be and how he created your physical beauty unique to you. Beauty involves taking care of yourself by living a healthy lifestyle, one that's balanced both internally and externally. You can use all of the fancy makeup and hair styling products in the world, but if you don't take care of yourself and find the confidence to stand tall, it won't matter.

Always remember, what's in your heart and mind is so much more important that what's on the outside. You aren't always going to impact others with a smoky eye, but you can easily impact others when you have a heart that is willing to serve. Forget about the latest makeup trends or the most expensive products. Embracing who you are, being confident, and sharing kindness with those others around you is truly the greatest beauty. As long as you're making who you are the priority, it can be a lot of fun to play with hair and makeup styles, and it's crucial to take good care of your skin and hair. Looking healthy, clean, and put together will never go out of style.

My beauty philosophy is to keep it simple and embrace the features you were given. In fact, I suggest finding your best feature and flaunting it. If you have a perfect pout, make sure you wear balms and glosses to highlight your lips. Do you have amazing curls? Find the right products and styling methods to show them off. It's so much easier to work with your natural features instead of against them. We all need to embrace our so-called flaws, our differences, and unique features. Embrace your quirks. They make you *you!* Freckles, glasses, braces, dimples—everything!

A lot of girls have insecurities about their bodies, skin, or their overall appearance. It's natural to go through periods of lower self-confidence or feeling uneasy in your skin. But don't wallow in it. Remember who you are and what you're capable of. You're not defined by a bad hair day, or a blemish, or eyeliner gone wrong. I want all the girls in the world to know that they are beautiful. I know that phrase gets thrown around a lot, and it can lose its power. But take this seriously: You. Are. Beautiful.

God made you in his image, and he knew exactly what he was doing when he created you.

Faith plays a big role in how I think about beauty. If I take pity on myself for looking bad, I'm not appreciating the beautiful person God made me to be. I want to be grateful for my healthy and capable body, so I should be thankful for my flaws and quirks too. That's all part of this beautiful package God created.

Once you know that—and I mean really know it, deep down—you can take everything else just a little less seriously. This is a great time in your life to experiment with different hair and makeup styles and to have fun with it all! When I'm looking for new ideas and tips, my first stop is YouTube. For both hair and makeup, I really love Jaclyn Hill, Chloe Morello, Kathleen Lights, and Carli Bybel. Their videos are packed with tips for cool new looks and products that inspire me.

There are so many aspects of beauty and taking care of yourself that it can be hard to keep track! From regular haircuts and manicures to tanning and teeth whitening, there many ways we can maintain and even improve our appearances. These activities can range from fun to torturous (hello, waxing!) and from inexpensive to break-the-bank.

I try to focus on details that will make a big difference, like painting my nails and making sure my skin is clean and healthy (facials are one of my beauty splurges). I've also learned that my eyebrows are one of my most important facial features . . . and maintaining them can be a real battle! Embrace your natural shape, but feel free to get them waxed, threaded, or tweezed if you need to. The first time I ever got my eyebrows done, I was sixteen, and I was amazed by the difference. The lady who did my brows simply took away all the unwanted strays and defined the shape—nothing crazy. Afterward, I was like, "Oh my gosh, those brows have been hiding under there for *how* long?!" I thought they looked fabulous. The secret to great brows is to rid of unwanted strays and clean up the shape, but don't over-pluck. For those of you with thinner or lighter brows, fill them in with a brow pencil, gel, or shadow one shade darker than your hair color so you can actually see them. You'll be amazed at how much your eyebrows will enhance the rest of your features.

A beautiful smile can go a long way too, and another great beauty trend is teeth whitening. Unfortunately, I have a couple teeth that broke a couple years ago while playing with my brothers in the pool, so I had to get ceramic caps put on the broken and chipped ones. Because of that, I've never whitened my teeth, but I know a lot of people who have. As long as you talk with your dentist to find a product that works for you, and you maintain good oral hygiene, you can get that smile sparkling.

SKINCARE

Clear, beautiful skin is something we're all chasing, but unless you're born with perfect genes, it can seem almost impossible to attain. Forget about perfect! Let's strive for healthy skin that is the best possible for you. Your skin is probably one of the first things people notice when they meet you, and it says a lot about your overall health and well-being. It's essential to develop good habits to take care of your skin.

Believe me when I say that good skin is not something I ever take for granted. I've suffered from constant breakouts for years, and it has been traumatizing. In fact, in ninth grade my acne got so bad that I didn't want to go to school! I felt so insecure about my skin that I wouldn't go anywhere without makeup.

Maintaining your skin and keeping it blemish-free takes a lot of effort and commitment. You have to try different products and regimes until you find the right combination that works for you. Then you have to stay consistent and keep it up, day in and day out. The end result is so worth it.

It's always embarrassing having a big pimple on your face, or for me, *lots* of pimples on my face. I always feel like people are looking at my skin and not *me* when I have a bad breakout. Trust me . . . makeup can help, but it can't fix everything. Caring for your skin comes first, and when you start a good routine, you'll find you need less makeup, not more.

Once, during freshman year when my skin was at its worst, I walked into the school bathroom, saw my face, and started crying. I was so embarrassed by the way I looked. I remember calling my dad and telling him that I felt so sick I had to go home. He picked me up, and I ran straight to my room and cried. I just wanted my skin to be clear.

Throughout most of high school, it seemed like none of my friends dealt with the same amount of acne that I had, and that made it difficult for me to talk to my friends about it. I felt like I tried everything—various face washes and different methods—and nothing worked. It really lowered my self-confidence when I didn't have makeup on. And even when I did have makeup on, I felt like people were staring at my face and all the makeup that I *would* wear. In the end, I had to remind myself that everyone deals with their own issues, whether it's their skin, their hair, their body, or something else entirely. I felt alone, but I wasn't alone, and I had to make sure I didn't let my negativity get the best of me.

> **TIP** A change in diet definitely helped my skin. When my skin is acting up, I stay away from dairy and foods with high sugar, and, after a few days, it usually clears up.

I still don't have perfect skin, but I've learned to accept my flaws and insecurities. Makeup got me through the worst of times when I was the most down on myself. And now that my acne isn't as bad, I don't have to worry about makeup all the time. I am so fine wearing zero makeup. I love it!

Most of the time you just have to experiment with products until you find the ones that react to your skin best. A good starting point is to identify what type of skin you have—normal, dry, oily, or combination. Then you can begin to choose products that work specifically for your type of skin. No matter what type of skin you have, acne can be an issue. I have used many different products trying to cure my acne. Some have worked and others haven't.

When you're looking for products to combat acne, you'll often find a lot of strong ingredients, including benzoyl peroxide and salicylic acid. These ingredients can be effective, but be careful not to use too much. Using too much of a strong product can be worse than using not enough. The same is true for any prescription creams. I've gone overboard with creams and it has completely dried out my face. It can be extremely painful, so take it from me and be cautious.

If you want to stay updated with my skincare routine, feel free to check out my YouTube channel. I love posting videos regarding skincare and beauty.

THE BASIC STEPS OF SKINCARE

Step 1: Wash your face every single morning and night with a gentle cleanser

It's important to wash your face when you get up and before you go to bed. But do NOT over-wash your face. I have made this mistake so many times. I would feel like the more I washed my face, the better, but it's actually worse for your skin if you constantly exfoliate and clean it. Let your skin rest and breathe.

Step 2: Exfoliate

I use a tough exfoliant every other day or every second day. This helps get all of the dead skin off my face and allows for a fresh and healthy layer of skin to breathe. There are many different exfoliants, which can work for all types of skin. You might need softer exfoliants if you have sensitive skin, and you might need a rougher scrub if you tend to have oily skin. Find the strength you like and use it accordingly for the best results.

Step 3: Wear sunscreen every day

We all know that too much sun exposure can seriously damage your skin—from sunspots and premature wrinkles to even dangerous skin cancers. The secret to beautiful skin for the long haul is to protect it from the sun's harsh rays. So wear your sunscreen, and wear it daily! There are so many options out there. Choose anything that works for you, but try to find one that has serious broad-spectrum coverage.

Step 4: Take off your makeup at the end of the day

Wash off your makeup before bed and before working out—no matter what! You should never go to bed with makeup on. Even though it can sometimes be the most annoying task when you get home from a long day, your skin will thank you in the long run. It's so important to strip all of that gunk off your face before you rest. Same thing with working out: You are going to sweat while you work out, which causes your pores to expand. You don't want all of your foundation to slip into your skin, causing even more breakouts.

Get makeup remover wipes that can remove all the makeup and dirt from your skin. I used to avoid taking off my makeup before bed because I was too lazy and tired, and I would always wake up with pimples on my face. Now, I force myself to wash everything off. I also keep a pack of makeup remover wipes in my car in case I make a spontaneous trip to the gym.

Step 5: Moisturize

Moisturizing your skin is important, and not only moisturizing with creams . . . hydrate your skin from the inside out! Drink lots of water for healthy, glowing skin. Your skin is going to thank you. Search "hydration calculators" online and, by answering a few quick questions, it will tell you approximately how much you should be drinking a day to keep your body healthy. I love using a gel-like moisturizer, such as ones from Simple and Cetaphil. They're both super lightweight, so I don't feel like I have a ton of product on my face. If you want something that is going to combat acne, you can try moisturizers that have salicylic acid in them.

And remember, skin is everywhere on your body, so take care of your whole body. I shower every day, and I love to take a bath once a week, sometimes with Epsom salts. The salt can relax your body and relieve any stress you might have in your muscles. If I'm not using Epsom salt, I enjoy using bath bombs or bubble baths for extra relaxation. Plus, who doesn't love a cute bubble bath?

After a shower or a bath, I always apply lotion. Applying your favorite body butter or cream all over your skin smells great and helps keep dry skin at bay. Moisturizing also goes hand in hand with exfoliating, and I like using exfoliating gloves or a loofa. Your skin will feel so much smoother after!

When it comes to skincare—whether it's your face or body— find a routine that works well for you, and stick to it. Patience is half the battle.

HOW TO DEAL WITH BREAKOUTS

- Wash your face in the morning and before bed with a gentle cleanser.
- Don't touch your face, and keep your hair off your face.
- Drink lots of water and eat well.
- No picking! Just let your skin be.
- Try a mask. Find one that is specifically for your skin type and what your skin needs.
- See a dermatologist. If your breakouts persist or get worse, it may be time to call in reinforcements. A dermatologist can help check for any underlying issues and will prescribe the right products or medication to get over the flare-up.

TIP No matter what you're dealing with, be confident and smile. Let your personality shine through. That's what people will see and remember about you, not your smudged eyeliner or the blemish on your chin.

MAKEUP

Makeup is a very creative product to play with. It's fun to create unique looks that are tailored for your face. It's amazing how a few simple products can transform a person's look completely.

Once I began getting into makeup, it was hard to wrap my head around how many different products and tools there are to use. It all seemed so glamorous, and there were so many fascinating creams, powders, and brushes. I learned a lot from just watching my mom, but I never applied makeup myself until I was in eighth grade, unless it was theater makeup for a show. When I was ready to wear my own on a daily basis, I had a lot to learn!

At first, I was terrible at applying makeup. I was always goofing up on the right shades to wear. I would wear concealer that was way too dark or way too light, and I would add way too much blush. I didn't even learn how to put on liquid eyeliner until a couple months ago.

No one really told me what to buy or what to get. I just saw products on YouTube that I really liked. I started out buying products from the drugstore, and then gradually began using higher-end makeup once I knew how to properly apply those products. You can find my favorite makeup must-haves in the

STOCK YOUR MAKEUP ARSENAL

The basic items you need to look awake, healthy, and put together are concealer (if you need it), blush, a highlight, and a good lip color. With those products in hand, you will have a beautiful glow. You don't need to buy expensive products or layer a lot on your face. Oftentimes, if I just want to add a little oomph to my look, I apply blush, a highlight, some pink lip balm, and I'm out the door. Those products add some color to my face, which makes me look awake and alive. You don't always need mascara, fancy eyebrows, and eyeliner for a good look. It's great to keep it simple; but at the same time, if you're in the mood, go full glam, girl!

Here are my favorite products in every category, just to give you something to refer to:

Foundation

Drugstore: Covergirl Outlast 3-in-1 Foundation
High End: Make Up For Ever Ultra HD Foundation

Concealer

Drugstore: Maybelline Instant Age Rewind Concealer
Drugstore: Maybelline Fit Me Concealer
High End: Make Up For Ever Camouflage Concealer

Blush

Drugstore: NYX blushes
High End: Tarte blushes

Mascara

Drugstore: L'Oréal Voluminous Mascara
High End: Benefit's They're Real Mascara

Highlight

Drugstore: Maybelline Master Strobe Stick
High End: Anastasia Beverly Hills Glow Kit palette, in Gleam

Bronzer

Drugstore: NYC Smooth Skin Bronzer
High End: Benefit's Hoola Bronzer

Eyeshadow

Drugstore: L'Oréal Color Riche La Palette in Nude
High End: Lorac Pro Palette

Powder

Drugstore: NYX Finishing Powder in Translucent
High End: Make Up For Ever HD Micro Finish Powder

TIP Keep a small cosmetic bag packed with your touch-up essentials in your schoolbag or purse. My must-haves throughout the day are concealer, lip balm, and a rollerball perfume. Other great items you can carry are small hand lotions, blotting papers if you have oily skin, and some emergency supplies like a Band-Aid and a safety pin.

sidebar, and I always keep my YouTube channel updated with new finds.

When it comes to makeup, less is more. I like to focus on playing up my best features and covering any blemishes. I'm not a huge trend follower. I know what works for my face and what I really like, so I tend to stick with what I know. Occasionally, I'll try out a new trend at home, but I usually don't wear it out. For example, I love the look of winged eyeliner on other girls. I've definitely experimented with that for fun, to see how it looks, but I love that my eyes look much bigger without eyeliner, so I prefer to stay away from it.

Test out natural colors first, but don't be afraid go for it. You'll learn what works best on you the more you play around with it.

MY EVERYDAY MAKEUP ROUTINE

I start by applying a moisturizer to create a healthy base for my makeup.

Second, I apply my foundation of choice with a beauty blender, which I wet slightly. A beauty blender is a pointed sponge that you dip into the foundation and then pat into your skin. That's right, pat—never rub! Bounce it on your skin like a bouncy ball bounces up and down.

Next, I grab concealer and apply it underneath my eyes to conceal any dark circles and blemishes I might have.

Then, I apply a light powder over my face so that my make-up sets and doesn't move throughout the day!

Next, I sweep a little bronzer, blush, and highlight on my face. I put my bronzer on the hollows of my cheeks, the blush on the apples of my cheeks, and the highlight on my cheekbones and any high point of my face.

Now moving on to eyes: I usually sweep some of the bronzer into the crease of my eyelids just to give a little definition. I then apply some highlight right on my brow bone and on the inner corners of my eyes to make me look super awake.

After my highlights are applied, I curl my lashes and apply some mascara.

Next, I comb through my brows and may or may not fill them in. Often, I just like my brows to be natural. I used to fill them in a ton when bold brows were trendy, but I love the way they naturally look.

Finally, I apply some lip balm, and that's it! I don't really love bold colors on my lips, because I like my natural lip color.

Sometimes I will apply a setting spray if I really want to lock everything in. Other times, I don't mind going without it.

TIP Wash your brushes or sponges. Left uncleaned, your makeup brushes and sponges can lead to major breakouts. Technically, you should wash them after every use, but it's probably more realistic to wash them once a week. Use a little antibacterial soap or a specifically made brush cleaner, along with warm water, to get rid of anything that might irritate your skin or cause breakouts.

You should wear whatever makeup makes you feel confident so that your inner beauty can shine through. If you want to rock a bold look, do it. If you want to go all natural, do that. It's your choice! There are no rules. Just have fun and enjoy experimenting with looks. But remember not to go too overboard in settings that don't allow it. In middle school, our principal had a no-makeup rule for the girls. If your school has the same rules, don't overstep the boundaries.

Every person has a unique look, and it's important to find what looks best for *you*. However, that doesn't mean you can't try what friends or celebrities are doing! Gigi Hadid and Selena Gomez are two huge beauty role models for me. I love every makeup and hair look they wear to red carpets and just around town. I don't want to be exactly like someone else, but those are two people I draw a lot of inspiration from. It's good to have fashion or beauty icons that you can look to when you're in need of some new ideas.

HAIR

I may keep it relatively simple when it comes to makeup, and I usually avoid jumping on any trendy bandwagons, but when it comes to hair, I love experimenting! I have had my hair super long, and then I have randomly cut it to my jawline. In fact, the first time we did the big chop, I forgot to mention it to my mom. She walked in mid-haircut, and her jaw dropped all the way down to the ground. It was quite the makeover. It's all about being spontaneous! I am not super attached to having my hair a certain way, so I love trying new styles.

The best thing you can do for your hair is keep it healthy. I recommend getting a trim every month or so, just to keep the overall shape of your style in place, the ends looking healthy, and to prevent damage. Find a shampoo and conditioner for your hair type, and check out post-shower nourishing oils to help your hair stay smooth and silky. I also love dry shampoo—it can be a lifesaver between washes!

I tend to be more of a hair-in-a-bun kind of gal when I'm running out to appointments or meeting up with friends, but when I want to look put together, I'll either curl or straighten my hair. I love to create loose beach waves with a curling iron, and for my audition on *The Voice*, I had this ultra-curled look. It's a style similar to how I wear my hair a lot, except the curls were a tad bit tighter. For my battle rounds, I knew it was time to step it up, so when I got in the chair to have my hair done, I just said to the stylist, "Let's do something cool with it!" She curled the ends of my hair, and then twisted sections along my hairline and put in these funky golden rings. The look made me feel so energized, and I used that attitude it gave me in my performance.

If I'm going out, I will curl my hair or do some light waves to give it some body. And sometimes, I'll pull it back in a really low, smooth bun. I think it looks classy and sleek. Those are my two go-to "going out" hair looks. Otherwise, I like to keep my hair down and natural or in a ponytail.

When you're planning your look for a formal event, use your hair to your advantage and let it show off your fashion. For example, if you're wearing an outfit with a high neckline or a dress with a beautifully designed back, pull your hair up so everyone can see the details.

DEVELOPING REAL STYLE

Style is a very personal thing, and it can communicate a lot about who you are. So whether you're fashion-forward or more laidback, you'll want to cultivate a look that conveys you're put together.

Express yourself through your clothing, and let your style be evident. There is a difference between being stylish and being trendy. Having style means you look pulled together and at ease in your clothes. It can be fun to try out a trend and add it to your usual look. Just make sure that your trends work for you and your body. For example, I love wearing high-waisted pants with a tighter top. This look cinches in my waist, shows off my curves, and accentuates my natural figure.

TIP It can be very intimidating to go into a salon and ask for a big change. Be prepared with pictures of styles you like and be confident in asking for what you want. My colorist, Debi Dumas, has been doing my hair since I was sixteen, and she also has been doing my mom's hair since she was my age. I feel so comfortable with her and completely trust her judgment. When I was first allowed to dye my hair, I went to her salon and told her what I wanted. We talked a lot about what tones we wanted to see and where to add highlights and lowlights. If you are feeling unsure about dying your hair, you can always go for a consultation at a hair salon. Get advice from someone who really knows about hair!

Find the cuts, styles, silhouettes, and shapes that you love on your body and build your wardrobe from there. You know you'll feel confident in those pieces, and then you can add a trendy item or accessory to mix it up.

When you're wearing an outfit that you love and that conveys your personality, you'll feel and even act more confident. This holds true if you're dressing for an important interview or special event, but you can also see the difference even when running errands. Don't throw on just any old thing because you don't know what to choose and the comfortable sweatshirt on your bedroom floor seems like an easy answer. Your style can have positive effects on many aspects of your life. When you look good, you feel good.

In addition to looking your best, it's important to make sure that you're representing yourself in a way that lines up with your values and beliefs. Modest is hottest. You can absolutely express yourself with your clothes without compromising your values. Don't go around wearing the shortest shorts and the smallest tops you can find. Having good style is better than wearing skimpy clothing. Be unique with your choices, but make sure they are honoring the things that you stand for.

TIP Some girls think they have to flaunt what they've got in tight or revealing pieces. You don't have to put it all on display to look beautiful, put-together, and yes, even attractive. Keep an air of mystery. Even if you have the best bod in the world, don't put it all on display.

HOW TO DEVELOP YOUR PERSONAL STYLE

- Do your research. Go shopping and make a note of what you like as you walk around. Don't buy it yet, but snap a picture to refer to later.
- Pay attention to celeb icons. Look at pictures of celebrity fashion and pull all of the images you like. What do they have in common? Structured, tailored pieces? Soft and feminine? Bold prints and colors?
- Compare your shopping snaps with the celeb references and make sure you're gravitating toward the right pieces when you shop. It's easy to get caught up in what the store is displaying prominently or what your friends like.
- Go shopping with a friend. I love bringing my mom or my friends when I shop, because they can give me a second opinion. I want someone to keep me accountable.

Accessorizing is a fun way to jazz up an outfit. I love adding statement belts, necklaces, and hats. They add a little personality to your look without looking overdone. In fact, my jewelry collection is mostly statement necklaces, and I like finding that one perfect piece to tie the whole look together.

Accessories can also be a good way to try out trends without having to spend a ton of money. Besides, I tend to lose all my jewelry unless it's latched around my neck, so I try not to spend too much on things that I know I won't be able to take care of. I'm trying to get better at it, though. One piece of jewelry at a time.

DRESS FOR THE OCCASION

While your personal style is all about expressing your individuality, you also want to dress appropriately for different situations. Wearing the right clothes for the occasion is a good way to ensure you feel confident and prepared. Wearing heels to an active date, for example, or a low-cut blouse to a job interview, are surefire ways to feel out of place and insecure.

Here are my style suggestions for a few classic situations:

First date

I think it depends on where you're going, but one go-to look is black jeans, a nice top, booties, and a jacket. It's cute and the right balance between casual yet dressy. Depending on where you're going, you can jazz up the outfit if you need to. If you're going mini golfing, be casual and replace the booties with cute sneakers. If you're going to a nice dinner, jazz it up with some jewelry. Be yourself and reflect who you are in your clothing. Don't wear something that isn't you!

First day of school

Keep it simple and cool! Wear a pair of great jeans, comfortable shoes, and a cute top. Don't overdress. You want to look effortlessly cool and not like you're trying too hard.

Interview

Wear something professional looking, and keep it modest. This isn't the time to bring out your short skirts and your low-cut tops.

Wear something that is going to reflect your maturity in the workplace. This also can vary depending on what type of job you are applying for. Let the position you're applying for dictate the clothing you wear. A collared blouse and even a blazer can work in many different settings, and you can keep it simple or go bold with accessories. If you're applying for an internship at a hip local magazine, add the funky necklace you found at a flea market to showcase your individuality. If you're applying for a job at a local financial company, keep the colors neutral and the jewelry minimal.

Party

Wear something that you feel confident in. I know some girls like to wear dresses and heels, while others like to wear jeans and boots. Wear whatever makes you feel the best. Don't forgot about comfort, though. It's hard to have a good time and laugh when you're constantly adjusting your clothes or sitting down because your feet hurt.

Hike with friends

I normally wear athletic shorts or leggings, a tank top, and running sneakers. I love getting a matching set with a coordinating sports bra and yoga pants. It makes me feel a little bit more pulled together. When being active, make sure you're wearing clothing that can get dirty and that allows you to move around without any problems.

Running errands

Keep it casual with jeans, cute sneakers, and a T-shirt. Nothing fancy when you're running around. Comfort is key.

As your style becomes more important and you seek out inspiration and references, you may begin to have some designer tastes. There are times to splurge on well-made pieces that you will love and wear for a long time, and times to save and buy inexpensive versions of the desired piece. And if you don't mind hand-me-downs, try swapping clothes with your friends. Trade a shirt or a dress for a month, or borrow something for a specific occasion. Most of my friends love doing this—we all get something new for a while without spending a cent.

> Nothing is more stylish that being a strong woman of faith, so focus on the inside first.

While you're saving up to buy an expensive item like a leather coat or chic booties, look for pieces that are classic and will never go out of style. Don't spend the money on a trendy look that you might get sick of next year. Choose a classic cut and a classic color like black, gray, navy, or burgundy. Make sure whatever you're buying fits well and is comfortable.

Style is such a personal thing. It can showcase your personality and your outlook on life. The most important parts of you are on the inside, like your faith, your creativity, your intelligence, and your sense of humor. How you look and how you dress can show the world who you are inside. So have fun with your style, your hair, and your makeup. But remember, nothing is more stylish that being a strong woman of faith, so focus on the inside first.

CLOSET MUST-HAVES

Every girl should be working toward adding these items to their closets, as they are must-have essentials for building a killer wardrobe. These classic pieces are worth keeping around season after season, so buy quality pieces and treat them well. They'll be the foundation for most of the outfits you wear.

- ☐ Denim jacket
- ☐ Ballet flats
- ☐ Blazer
- ☐ Leather jacket
- ☐ Black booties
- ☐ Cute sneakers
- ☐ Perfectly fitting jeans
- ☐ Statement necklace
- ☐ Well-fitted bra
- ☐ Black dress
- ☐ White T-shirt
- ☐ Opaque black leggings

CHAPTER 9

FAITH IN REAL LIFE

To pray is to let go and let God take over.

PHILIPPIANS 4:6–7 (PARAPHRASE)

May the God of hope fill you with all joy and peace as you trust in him, so that you may overflow with hope by the power of the Holy Spirit.

ROMANS 15:13

Each person's story of faith is unique to that person. In Sunday school, and sometimes while talking with friends at school, I heard the story of how they asked Christ into their life. I've heard some talk about going to church with a friend and being overwhelmed when they heard about how much God loved them. Other stories were about going to a Christian summer camp or praying with their parents at home. The same is true for what faith and being a Christian has meant to their life and how it has changed them.

I want to talk to you about what real faith can mean for your life, but to do that, I want to share my story with you first. My story came to be largely because I grew up in a Christian family who believed it was important to teach my brothers and me that God created us and loves us.

MY STORY OF FAITH

I remember the first time I accepted the Lord into my heart. I was six years old. During the regular Sunday morning service, the youth pastor asked if anyone wanted to accept Jesus into their heart, and if they did, to close their eyes and say a prayer aloud. This question wasn't asked every week, but it was asked regularly, and for some reason I felt led to respond on this particular day. After saying that prayer, I honestly felt like I was on top of the world. I wanted to be closer to God, and it was an important step in furthering my relationship with him.

I took it very seriously. I went home that day and I asked my mom if I was "being a good Christian." Since I had accepted the Lord into my heart, I thought that I had to act perfect. And if I didn't, then I clearly wasn't a Christian. So I would ask my mom all the time, "How am I doing? Am I still being a Christian?" I must have asked her so many times that I started to annoy her. But she sat me down and told me that being a Christian isn't about "being good." It's about acknowledging that we are sinners living in a sinful world, unable to become right with God on our own merits. So God sent his one and only son, Jesus Christ, to come down from heaven, live a perfect life on earth, and pay for our sins by sacrificing himself for us and dying on the cross. Three days later, Jesus rose from the grave and now sits at the right hand of God, who has prepared a place for us in heaven. Having a relationship with Jesus and making disciples of every nation was what "being a Christian" was about. After understanding that, I looked at it in a completely new light.

A TIME OF DARKNESS

There was a specific time during my ninth-grade year when I went through a really tough time. I was dealing with some dark emotions. I had a bad attitude, was making poor decisions, and I wasn't living my life for Jesus. I just wasn't myself. I don't even quite know how to explain it, other than it felt like Satan had a hold of my heart. I felt angry

> Being a Christian isn't about "being good."

and sad. I felt numb, like I didn't care about anything. I didn't even have anything in particular to be mad at or upset about. I wasn't feeling rebellious, but more like I didn't care about anything, and I wanted to be by myself. It felt much easier to be mad and to have a bad attitude than to try to be happy and be outgoing when I wasn't feeling like it.

I began to make bad decisions—everything from lying about where I was going to saying mean and hurtful things to my brothers, and being disrespectful to my parents by not following the house rules and having a major attitude whenever I spoke to them. Even I knew I was being a jerk, but I couldn't get out of my funk . . . I had a cloud over my head and a sulky face on all the time. I couldn't find the sunshine in my life anymore and didn't want to be a part of my family, to be nice, to be happy, to be positive. Not that I was always upbeat before that, but I'd generally been a happy person. But now I suddenly felt lost and angry and alone, and those feelings made me want to isolate myself even further.

I was not reading the Bible, praying, or listening to God. I blocked him out. I didn't want to listen to the advice of my parents or receive the love of my family. My life felt so dark that I just continued to spiral down emotionally, and I didn't know how to stop myself.

My poor parents were trying to get through to me, to understand what I was going through and help put me back on the right track, but I didn't know how to express myself and really didn't want to talk about it. They knew that I was in a really bad, funky place in my life, and they just wanted me to be the Natasha they knew and loved. They wanted to see me smiling again. It hurt them when I would make bad decisions. They knew I was going through something and didn't want to have to punish and discipline me for my poor choices, but they had established our family rules and I wasn't following them. They had to follow through with consequences if I wouldn't open up and let them in to help me. And believe me, most of the things I did deserved those consequences, like being grounded, or getting my phone and computer taken away. I would have many conversations with my mom about trying to turn my attitude around and understanding why I was acting out in anger so much. I honestly still don't know. Nothing secretly happened to me that I wasn't sharing. My emotions just took over for the worse. I put my parents through so much, things I'll keep between the three of us for now, and I felt bad knowing that they only wanted to help me feel like myself again.

Finally, the light broke through the darkness. At the end of my freshman year, my mom and dad decided to send me to a Christian summer camp outside of Branson, Missouri, called Kanakuk. My mom sprung this "camp idea" on me just after I finished finals, and I was not happy about it. At the time, I was going to therapy every week to try to express my feelings and release some of the emotional darkness that had consumed me. I felt like I was finally getting to a place where I was getting better, happier even. I had a better relationship with everyone in my family, and I genuinely felt like things were looking up. When my mom told me I was going to Missouri, I became very angry again. I didn't want to go. She told me I was going to be away for an entire month. I was freaking out. I didn't know one single person at this camp. I didn't know anything about it, and I was going by myself?! I fought her every moment.

MORE THAN A CAMPING TRIP

The day came for me to leave for camp, and I still was very angry with my parents. I had no idea what to expect. I packed a trunk full of clothes, toiletries, and bug spray, and flew by myself to Missouri. I didn't even have my cell phone, because my mom read that cell phones weren't allowed at camp. She didn't realize we could drop them at the main office until camp was over, so she made me leave it at home. I think she was as nervous to send me off as I was to go. She checked on my flight, called the camp to make sure I found the camp bus at the airport, and again to know I had arrived safely.

Kanakuk is located on Table Rock Lake, and is surrounded by woods and fields in what seemed like the middle of nowhere. Scared and unsure, I unpacked my stuff in a cabin along with ten other girls I'd never met, and let me tell you, it was not what I expected *at all*! It was the best month of my life! We went cliff jumping, jet skiing, and wakeboarding. We played tennis and volleyball, and did archery. Our days were filled with running and playing and enjoying the beautiful outdoors together, getting tan, and telling each other our life stories. We even spent a night in a cave that was filled with bats. Sounds scary, but it was so cool. Another night we slept on the sand of a secluded beach and spent the next day on a boat.

All of the friendships I made during my weeks at camp were meaningful and incredible because almost everyone had at least one thing in common—a love and desire to live for Jesus Christ. Everyone was in a different place in their walk with the Lord, but we were all there trying to strengthen that relationship. Our nights were filled with talks called "K-Life." We would go into an open room with a stage, and leaders of the camp like Joe White, Adam Donyes, and Don Ford would pour into us. The night would start off with worship led by some of the counselors.

SONGS MEANT MORE

Singing out to Jesus and being surrounded by some of your best friends is the coolest experience. The time of worship is so important to me, and one of the ways I feel like I can tell God how much I love him. Oftentimes, I get very emotional because it hits my heart so hard, and the words that I'm singing are to praise his name.

After the worship time was over, we would sit down and listen to the night's speaker. The topics would vary each night. Some of the talks had a theme like purity, creation, and social

PUT THAT JOURNAL TO USE

SONGS ARE MORE THAN JUST MUSIC

Have you ever written down the words to your favorite worship song? What do they say? What touches you the most and why? Songs can bring us closer to God than we could ever imagine.

My favorite song to worship to is "You're Beautiful" by Phil Wickham. I cry every single time I hear it. The lyrics are so close to my heart and make me feel so connected to the Lord when I sing with all I have. There is a lyric that says "I see you there hanging on a tree. You bled and then you died and then you rose again for me. Now you are sitting on your heavenly throne. Soon we will be coming home." Those words remind me that this earth is not our home. Our home is with him up in heaven. What we have right now is only temporary.

media. Other K-Life nights were based around Scripture. We would dive deep into the Word and uncover the meaning of what God is trying to tell us. I would always bring my journal to K-Life and write about the things being said so that I could reflect and look back at them later.

TRUSTING GOD TO LEAD

The counselors and the staff were vessels that the Lord placed for me to learn more about him. I remember having some heart-to-heart conversations with my counselors that, quite frankly, were not always easy. I got asked some hard-hitting questions about how I was and where I was at in my life. It probably would have been easier to shelter myself from the questions and brush them away, but I unleashed. I had to be honest with myself and verbalize where I was at—and it wasn't a great place. That's all a part of growing. Being honest with myself was something that I had to work on. Understanding that things weren't great in my life and that I needed change was something that *had* to happen in my life in order for things to be different. I am so grateful that I was able to have those tough conversations with the counselors, because without addressing the problems, how could I move forward?

If you have someone you look up to spiritually, ask questions! Have those hard-hitting conversations about where your life is at and how you can stay or get on the right track. Those same counselors, still to this day, will call me and text me, asking the same questions. They ask me if I am in the Word every day. They ask me if my priorities are straight. They ask me if things have been shaky. Not all the answers I give are going to be positive, but that's okay. Having someone you can talk to and get encouragement from will help strengthen the path you're on toward creating a more intimate relationship with God.

We learned so much about who God really is and how he can radically change our lives during these talks and moments of fellowship. Hearing this day in and day out changed me completely. God opened my eyes to things that I had never seen or heard. More importantly, he opened my heart. He placed new people in my life that summer who drastically impacted me, my spirit, and my soul. I will never forget that summer because it changed me forever. I know I would not be who I am today without that month of Kanakuk.

GOING HOME

I came home a completely different girl after that month of camp. Family members noticed it too, which made me so happy! I was in sync with my faith and feeling good about my behavior. I'm so grateful my mom and papa knew what I needed to get back on track and reconnect with the Lord. They told me later that they didn't just send me on a whim, but had been praying for several months about how to help me. Over a four-day period, three different people told them about Kanakuk without them even asking about a camp or knowing what I was going through. My parents saw that as confirmation that Kanakuk was the place I needed to go, and knew it was an answer to their prayers.

Transferring the things I learned to my life back home was difficult, though. Maybe you've had a similar experience: You are surrounded by Jesus-loving friends and mentors for a month straight, and then you go back to your hometown that is filled with lots of people with different outlooks on life. It's not always easy to live out life the same way you did at camp. They call this the "Kamp High" at Kanakuk. Each time I go to Kanakuk, I come home and am so excited to share Jesus with all my friends and implement things I learned at camp. It lasts for a little while, and then I begin to go back to old habits, such as not picking up the Bible daily, conforming to the ways of the world, and not living the life that I was living when I was at camp.

That's why it's so important to have friends, family, and mentors to keep you accountable. Stay in the Word every day. Pray and communicate with God as much as you can. Find a devotional you can read in the mornings, or even before you go to bed. There are apps out there, such as "Sprinkle of Jesus," that send about five notifications each day with Scripture or little snippets of wisdom. Stick with God, because he's not going anywhere.

A FAITH OF YOUR OWN

It might not be a camp that changes everything for you. It might be the conversation you have with your pastor. It could be a sermon you hear on the radio. Whatever it may be, allow the change in your life to influence you for the better and strive to be a light! Live out the words that you want to follow. Don't just hear them once and then sit at home. Get active and follow the lifestyle you want to live.

People can see the difference when Jesus is in your life. Having a relationship with the Lord has changed me so much. It has changed my heart and how I look at the world. It's also nice to have friends who share the same faith as me, because we can encourage each other, and I love that! They push me to be a stronger Christian.

HE'S THERE IN EVERY PAIN AND EVERY JOY

No matter what you're going through and how hard it seems, God is there. He is there to hold your hand through the trials and tribulations in your life. Sometimes it can be hard to understand why certain things happen to people that lead to heartbreak, but it's important to remember that God has a plan. It may be hard to see or figure out the plan, but with prayer and petition, he will see through everything in your life. He will never forget about you during times of pain, and certainly won't forget about you even when you feel like everything is fine in your life. It's easy for me to get upset when things don't go my way, and to turn to God and question what he's doing. Why would he allow these things to happen in my life? It's all part of a plan, I know, and I wish I knew what that plan is, because I don't. But I can wake up every morning and do my best to trust that the outcome of living for him is better than anything.

FAITH & FAMILY

Just like my family, my faith is one of the most important parts of my life, and it's something I strive to honor. Being led by God at all times is at the very core of who I am and how I act. My parents are the inspiration for my beliefs, and I'm encouraged by how they live according to those principles each and every day. My whole family—not only my parents and brothers, but grandparents, aunts, uncles, and cousins—have been important examples and role models for me in my faith journey. I realize I am fortunate that most of my extended family are Christians who walk with God. It's that connection between faith and family that can help people live a life that honors the Lord.

It makes my journey easier as well, because there are many faithful people around me to talk to, answer my questions, and guide me when theology gets confusing. Maybe some of you have families like mine, but I know that others may not know one single Christian in their life. Don't worry, you're not alone, because now you know me.

HOW TO TALK TO GOD

Building a direct relationship with God is important when it comes to honoring and serving him. Here are some ways to get back into talking to God, or perhaps even starting for the first time:

- **It's not about where you are.** You don't have to be in a church or at Bible study to talk to God. He's always there with you. When you need him, or when you feel him urging you, just start talking.
- **Tell him about everything.** Just like writing in your journal, talking to God is a chance to talk about anything and everything in your life—your frustrations, worries, excitement, hopes, and even your crushes. (If there's anyone you should be talking to about love and who you will spend your life with, it's God!)
- **Don't be afraid.** If you're nervous at first, think of prayer as a conversation and start talking as you would talk to a friend.
- **Set aside time.** Make time to sit in a quiet room with no distractions and open your mind and heart. If you're anxious or your mind is stuck on something else, take a minute to calm down before you pray. You can even ask God to quiet your heart and focus your mind on him. He's the ultimate helper!
- **Write it out.** Make a prayer list of those you want to pray for. You can also try a prayer guide with some suggested topics that are important to you and your family as a way to get started.
- **Remember to listen too.** Have you ever gone to a coffee

shop at its busiest time and tried to have a private conversation with a close friend? It just doesn't feel right. Any good conversation is about both talking and listening, so remember to let God respond. He often speaks to us in the quietness of our heart, so we need to give him space to talk.

Whether you have these influences in your life or not, you will face issues that you'll wrestle with. I struggle each and every day with temptations and desires that the Lord tells me to steer clear of. I have my family to help guide me, but that doesn't mean that I'm perfect as a result. I'm constantly faced with adversity, whether it be with lying, boys, family, or emotions. The only one who can help me overcome these things completely is God.

GROUNDED IN FAITH

Both of my parents were introduced to the Christian faith at a young age, but it wasn't until they were married that they really delved into their faith. They are both spiritual leaders in our household as well as among their friends, and I'm happy to have examples like that. My mom wanted to raise us in a Christian household, so from the time my brothers and I were born, we started learning about God, both at home and in church. Sunday school was super fun, and full of friends and wonderful teachers who filled the church with a strong sense of love and community.

My parents taught me how important it was to have a direct relationship with the Lord. I would pray to God regularly throughout the day: before meals, anytime I was having a bad moment at school, and with my parents at night before bed. My mom and papa told me that the only way to eternal life in heaven is through Jesus.

My mom inspires my faith the most. She represents him in everything that she does, and that really does set an example for me. You can see the light of the Lord in her. It's noticeable. She is such a strong woman and inspires me to be a warrior of faith!

SUPPORTING EACH OTHER

Although God has always been present in my family, it's not to say that we haven't strayed or questioned our faith at different times. Just like we all grow and change, so does our faith and relationship with God. God is *always* there, waiting to have a relationship with us. He never leaves, but waits patiently for us to join him and rejoin him, again and again, every day.

Even though I try my best to live my life in a way that honors God, it doesn't mean I don't sin. Everyone does, and everyone makes mistakes. We wouldn't be human if we didn't. That's why we need Jesus in the first place. His righteousness—meaning he is perfect and holy—covers over the mistakes we make when we aren't in line with God's Word. We know what God's Word says by reading it daily. A family based in faith is such a huge support in bringing us back to God and being there when we fall.

> God is *always* there, waiting to have a relationship with us.

When I was turning away from God, my family and friends played a huge role in boosting me up when I didn't know what to do. They were right there to help me pick up the broken pieces and start to live a life according to his Word. It's not easy going through trials and tribulations, but having a family who loves me and wants me to have a close relationship with Christ was what I needed to get back in the right place. I even remember being at camp and having moments of emotional breakdown, when the girls in my cabin would comfort me. They were there to pick me up when I was at my lowest point.

FACING TEMPTATION

Keeping your faith in a world that does not always support it or make it easy can be a challenge, but it's part of the journey. Being a teenager is typically filled with a lot of new experiences, important social interactions, new friendships, possible relationships, and the pressure to fit in with your peers. Staying true to yourself and your beliefs can be tough. I would much rather feel good about my decisions and know that my heavenly Father is proud of the actions that I make.

There have been many times when I felt torn, pulled in two directions by what I want in the moment or what my friends are doing and what I know is right. I'm tempted all the time, and it's in those times that I look to God and say, "*Help!*" The coolest part is when he answers. I don't actually hear his voice audibly, but I can hear his voice within me. Some people call it your conscience, intuition, or a gut feeling. But when you've received Jesus as your savior, God says that he sends a helper for you, the Holy Spirit, who will guide you, nudge you, and whisper those things you know to be true and right into your heart and mind. To make sure it really is the Holy Spirit talking, you want to be

FOCUS ON FAMILY TOGETHERNESS

Help your family create quality time to just be together and to share in your relationship with God. Your parents will lead the way as the heads of the household, but it can be rewarding to suggest some of these activities and encourage your siblings to make the time. Go on a family bike ride, and when you reach your destination, do a devotional. Spend time in fellowship together. Listening to Christian podcasts in the car can also be entertaining and extremely educational. My papa is a huge fan of podcasts and loves listening to sermons in the car as a family. Another fun way to get connected with your family is the "pasta pot prayer" idea. Everyone in your family takes a piece of paper and writes down some prayer requests that they have. Everyone folds up their papers and puts them into the center of the table. Next, shuffle them like you would mix up pasta in a pot. Each family member then grabs a sheet of paper, and whoever's paper you get is the person you can be praying for during the next week. Even doing something as simple as going out to breakfast as a family and bringing your Bible to read from can be impactful.

Here are some other ways to build faith as a family:

Create a mission statement. Sit down together and brainstorm your family's most important values and practices. Focus on your spiritual goals and commitment to church, as well as how you want to live and embody those ideals as a family. Think about how you want to treat each other and the kind of household you want to live in. Make sure the words you choose help remind your family of the faith and love you want to live out.

Play together. Find an activity that everyone loves to do and make the time to do it regularly. It can be athletic, like hiking or biking, or calmer activities, such as playing a board game or going out for ice cream. Every Saturday night, my family and I go out for sushi at a restaurant near our house and then we go get frozen yogurt. When we get home, we always watch a movie together or play board games. Those times are carved out for my family, and I love spending time with them. Sundays are also a day we spend together. We go out for Sunday morning breakfast at our local farmers' market and then head off to church. We love going on hikes together, as well as morning walks. It starts our day off by being active and also being together. And as long as everyone is actively engaged—that means phones off and distractions to a minimum—it's a great way to build quality time that keeps us feeling close.

Pray together. Find time to pray together with your family every day. If you're all busy, it can be as simple as a few minutes together, reading a short Bible verse from a devotional and discussing its importance. When you pray with your family, you create a sense of intimacy while you're all bowing your heads in reverence toward the Lord. Focus on being grateful, on forgiveness, and on your needs not just as an individual but also as a family. Almost every day, my family reads and discusses a passage from the Bible, led by my papa. We always pray together before meals; it's an easy reminder (because we all have to eat, don't we?) before we leave in the mornings and before bed. It's also a great way to come together in fellowship and focus on God's Word.

Celebrate. Take every opportunity to celebrate your family's accomplishments. Anything from a good grade on a big test, to graduation from any grade, and of course birthdays are opportunities to celebrate together.

certain the words or feelings you're hearing are consistent with God's Word. If the two things contradict each other, then you know the feelings you're having are deceiving you, or you may be trying to will the answer that you want to hear rather than what you need to hear. Sometimes my heart takes over and I don't make the right decisions. I'm human; I make mistakes. I've learned from many of them. But even then, I still fall into the nature of sin. It's not easy to combat sin all the time even if we have read Scripture and pray. You can't argue with the Bible; it doesn't change and it's always right. So when you're facing temptation, prayer and Scripture should be your go-to weapons. God always provides a way out.

Temptation is such a problem. I have struggled with temptation at so many different times and in so many ways, sometimes with boys, food, school, and my emotions. And I still do! If you fall into temptation and let go of your principles because of momentary weakness, you're cheating yourself. When you face those times, where it's hard to follow what God has said, pray. A great way to pull yourself back from the edge of temptation

SIX WAYS TO BEAT TEMPTATION

1. **Identify your temptations.** Be aware of what kinds of situations and people tempt you to make poor decisions. Be honest with yourself about your weaknesses. Memorize the Ten Commandments—make a quick-reference list in your head that reminds you of the main rules God gives for walking with his guidance. It is especially important to know the foundational guidelines God gave us in the Ten Commandments so you understand how temptation may be trying to get the best of you. There are visual tools as well you can find online that will help you memorize the commandments. That's what I used.

2. **Know who you can go to.** Share your temptations with a trusted friend, adult, or youth pastor who you can rely on to support you and help you stay strong in potentially risky situations.

3. **Talk and pray.** Once you identify your temptation, pray each and every day to find the strength to overcome it or avoid it. Also, try discussing what you're facing with your parents or your Bible study group. Together brainstorm ways to avoid this temptation.

4. **Have a couple go-to verses.** Find a couple Bible verses that speak specifically to what you're dealing with and memorize them. If you're constantly feeling the temptation to copy a classmate's homework or test, or you find yourself struggling with respecting your parents' rules, find some key verses you can repeat in those moments. They will give you the boldness to face anything you're going through. God's Word is a point of strength, so hide it in your heart. And remember: "I can do

all things through Christ who strengthens me" (Philippians 4:13, NKJV).

5. **Have an accountability partner.** Find a friend you trust, who you know is strong in their faith. Having someone to talk to when you're feeling tempted or weak can help you find strength when faced with difficult situations. You can encourage each other and know someone is praying for you. For me, my brothers are always there to keep me in check and support me in difficult situations. For you, this may be a friend at church who shares some of the same struggles.

6. **Walk away.** I wouldn't normally suggest avoiding your problems, but in the case of serious temptations, often the best thing to do is to avoid the situation altogether. If you know that going to a certain party or hanging out with a certain group of people is going to put you in a situation you're uncomfortable with, then make other plans. Or if you have a crush on a guy and you're not ready or allowed to date, or he's already in a relationship, it may be best to keep your distance. Not to say you can't be friends, but don't compromise yourself or others. Don't be afraid to walk away.

is finding someone to keep you accountable. I have a couple friends who keep me accountable for my actions and who want to see me succeed. They are going to be up front and honest with me if something isn't looking too great.

TEMPTATION BEYOND FAITH

Only a couple of my close friends actually share the same Christian beliefs as me. Some of my best friends are atheist, Buddhist, or Jewish. Even though we don't share the same beliefs, we can and do respect each other.

Staying true to your faith and what you believe is right is important whether you're Christian or not, or even if you claim a religion at all. You know who you are and what you're comfortable doing, so don't let others persuade you to do something you're not comfortable with. Find your moral compass, consider how you want your actions to represent you, and do your best to act accordingly.

SEEK AND QUESTION

There are certain times in life that are harder than others to keep your faith; but remember that during those tough times, even when you can't imagine it, God is seeing you through. God always has a plan, and I never doubt that plan for me, even when

TIP While it's amazing to have friends from all walks of life, having a few close friends who are also Christians can help you in many ways. They support you in tough moments when you're faced with temptation by helping keep you accountable to God. Your Christian friends can provide spiritual support when you're struggling. But more than that, their advice comes from the same biblical foundations of faith that you share.

it's hard to see or hear. Especially since we live in a world where we get criticized for what we believe in, it's important to stay strong. Know that God invites us to ask questions and search his Word to find answers. Stay true to what the Lord tells you and the plans that he has for your life.

WHAT'S THE POINT OF ALL THESE RULES?

Some of us think about what we can't do when we think about the Bible. It's true that there are some dos and don'ts. But let me remind you, as I constantly I remind myself—they are all there

TIP What about the parts of the Bible that can be tough to read and accept? Our society changes so fast, and Christian beliefs are challenged all the time. It's important to listen and pray about everything you read and learn as you study the Bible. Talk to God and express how you're feeling so that he can give you wisdom. There have been many days when I felt like I had so many questions about the Bible and what is says: How can this *all* be true? Does this even make sense? How can this be applied to today's times? I don't have all the answers, but I try to turn to someone who is much more knowledgeable than I am in this subject. My youth pastor, my camp counselors, and even my parents can give me a better understanding and help me navigate through the questions that often run through my mind.

for our own good and to bless us. Just like my parents give me rules because they love me, so does God, our Heavenly Father.

How many times have your parents handed you a list of rules? Maybe you were going out with some friends or having friends over, and they gave you a list of dos and don'ts. You sigh because you feel like you can handle it, but the rules are there to make sure you know what to do. The Bible does the same for us in the Ten Commandments. You probably know most of them already, such as, Don't lie, Don't steal, Don't murder ... Oh, and of course the one my parents made sure we memorized—Honor your father and mother. Those rules are actually there to show us that none of us are perfect. Not one. I don't know anyone who hasn't told a lie; do you? So what's the point? Because none of us are perfect, we need someone who is.

When you dive deeper into the Bible, you can see exactly what God tells us to stay away from. So much of what the Bible provides us is the guidance we need to serve God well and realize how we should live and interact with each other.

GROWING THROUGH THE QUESTIONS

Faith is as rewarding a journey as you make it. Your spiritual growth is a path that you'll walk your entire life, and your relationship with God begins now as you learn more about the Bible and begin to ask questions that put you on a path to investigate, learn, and wrestle with the specific information and tenants. It's important to engage and participate.

I think it's extremely important to research, learn, and get informed about the religion you stand by. Faith is a component of religion, but I encourage you to learn more about what you

FAITH SITUATIONS AND SOLUTIONS

SITUATION: I'm feeling unsure about my faith. What should I do?

SOLUTION: Talk to someone who shares the same faith and ask questions. Any time I am feeling unsure about something, I ask my mom. That isn't to say that the person you are going to go to will have *all* the answers, but I'm sure that he or she can help guide you. Don't be afraid to have conversations with people about faith and the things that you're doubting or struggling with. Talk to a youth pastor at your church or maybe a small group leader in your Bible study.

SITUATION: I'm a religious person, but I'm also feeling tempted to have sex with my boyfriend, which is at odds with my beliefs. What should I do?

SOLUTION: No matter how religious we are or how strong our beliefs are, we will all be tempted to have sex at some point. Sex isn't bad, but God does say it's reserved for marriage. I guess my question back to you is, are you choosing not to have sex because it's a rule you have to follow, or because your heart's desire is to honor God? It may seem like the same thing, but it's very different. Rules can always be broken, but conviction is a firmly held belief—one that the Holy Spirit can help you with if your desire is to please God. If you don't want to have sex, tell your boyfriend, and ask that he respects your wishes and doesn't encourage you to go farther than you want. This seems simple, but one way to help yourself stay strong is by not going into rooms where you can shut the door or be out of sight from others.

SITUATION: How do I reconcile with God after making a mistake?

SOLUTION: Repent by praying and asking God for forgiveness. The cool thing about God is that when we've asked him to be the Lord of our life, his forgiveness has already covered our mess. God knows we aren't perfect, and we will continue to make mistakes. But there isn't any mistake that is too big for God to forgive. Asking for forgiveness isn't just a confession to him, but an act of genuine remorse and an act of turning away from that mistake. It doesn't mean you may not make the same mistake again, but if it becomes a pattern or a habit, you probably haven't truly repented. Don't be afraid to talk to him about anything you want. Even if it's that you don't know how to stop doing the things you don't want to do. He knows your heart and your mind, and he will recognize your genuine plea for answers.

SITUATION: How can I talk to my friends about my religion if they're either a different religion or not religious at all?

SOLUTION: I love talking to my friends about Christianity, especially if they don't believe in the same things that I believe. It gives me an opportunity to share the love of Christ with them. Sometimes the topic of religion comes up organically, so it's an easy opening to jump in and ask them what they believe. Even if you already know the answer, it's a gentle approach to get them talking first, and it gives you a natural time afterward to share your faith. If religion never comes up in conversation, you sometimes just need to be bold and throw the question out there: *Do you believe in God?* You might be surprised how willing your friends will be to answer and enjoy the discussion. Remember, you don't have to have all the answers about your faith in order to talk about it. If you don't know the answer to a question they ask, just say, "I'm not sure. But I'll find out and get back to you." You don't have to convince them, convert them, or prove anything, only share with them. You're planting a seed. There will more opportunities to water it along the way.

SITUATION: There's a lot going on in the world that's bad, dangerous, and evil. How could God create that, as well as all of the good and beauty?

SOLUTION: This question can oftentimes lead you down the rabbit hole of millions of questions. I would advise asking someone like your pastor or mentor about this. What I've been told, and believe to be true from the Bible, is that the world was perfect before Adam and Eve ate the forbidden fruit in the Garden of Eden. Sin then entered the world. God gives us the choice: to stay in our sin or to live a life that honors and pleases him. God doesn't program us to be robots; he allows us to make our own decisions. He is always here to guide us through his Word, the Bible, and to help us live a Christ-centered life. But it is our choice whether to follow that guidance through our actions or not.

believe in—the theology of it. Anything that is as important to you as your faith is something you should know a lot about and spend time studying.

It's important for me to read the Bible, study it, and learn from my pastor. I need to be in the Word every day and keep God's words close to my heart. There have been so many times when I feel like I can't read the Bible because I don't understand it. The words can be tricky and I just tend to give up. Even now, I like reading from a children's Bible, or reading it with someone who can decode the words for me.

If you're struggling with the meaning of the Bible, there are other books, like devotionals. Some of my favorites are the devotionals with passages of Scripture along with a few para-graphs explaining the passage. To me, that is very helpful. It's a great way to start my morning. It sets up how I plan on acting toward people, how I go about my day, and the attitude I'm going to have.

Even though I don't always understand, I just keep working at it and making the effort. Don't give up when you're faced with a challenge. Daily engagement with the Bible and asking big questions are the things that help you grow in your knowledge of God, make you a stronger person of faith, and make the journey worth traveling.

Despite the tensions in the world that revolve around reli-gion, true Christianity is a powerful force for love, forgiveness, unity, charity, and grace. Actions speak louder than words. If you want to show people that Christ lives inside you and inspires you to love others the way he loves us, then show them through your actions. Show them through your kindness, joyful spirit, and the good work you do. Invite them to your church events or gather-ings so they can feel the warmth of the community. One of my biggest pet peeves is people who say they are one thing but act completely different. Be true to your word, and if you say you are something, act like it. Show who you are through the things you do and the way you uphold yourself.

You're capable of big things in your life and in your community, and maybe even in the world. While it's easy to feel like one small person who can't make a difference, you have to remember that it's possible, and it's particularly possible through the Lord. Live your life well and according to your faith, and even if you encourage just one person to do the same, you're making a bigger impact than you realize.

Anything is possible. The smallest effort of positivity and love can make a difference. Encourage others and be a light to people. Don't let the hate in the world consume you. Instead, be the light that outshines it!

CHAPTER 10

BE TRUE TO YOURSELF

*Charm is deceptive, and beauty is
fleeting; but a woman who fears the LORD
is to be praised.*

PROVERBS 31:30

When I was going through my early teen years, I wish I had known that if I had a better, more positive attitude, I would have been much happier. Instead, I felt alone in whatever I was dealing with, which pushed me to get stuck in negative thoughts. I wish I had known I didn't have to fit in with everyone else—that instead I needed to be true to myself. And more than anything, I wish I'd realized that all I needed was to trust and have faith in God.

LET'S BE REAL

The number one lesson I hope you'll take away from this book and my stories is the importance of being your authentic, true, *real* self. Remember who you are and what you believe in. Put it out there. Be confident in who you are, no matter the mistakes or setbacks you encounter. Lean on your friends, and be there for them when they need it.

Sometimes it can be hard to open up and share your experiences, heartbreaks, and embarrassing issues if you're not feeling good about yourself and confident in who you are. Go back to chapter one and work on building a strong identity and acting in accordance with your values. It's an ongoing process, so it's important to always be in touch with yourself and check in to make sure your decisions and actions are in line with your beliefs. We all get busy with school, jobs, friends, and family, and it can be difficult to set goals and work to achieve them. But I urge you to break out of the rut and work to better yourself. If you're not happy with who you are, if you want change—only you can make it happen!

That's what this journey is all about: knowing where you are, where you want to go, and being brave and strong enough to work hard. If you want to change something about yourself or your life, it starts with you. No one can do it for you.

At this point, you've identified who you are and what's important to you. You've strengthened your relationships with your friends and family, and learned how to take good care of yourself inside and out. Now, you need to practice consistency and live that way every single day.

> That's what this journey is all about: knowing where you are, where you want to go, and being brave and strong enough to work hard.

LOVE YOURSELF

To love yourself means to accept and respect yourself for who you are. Of course, it's good to have goals and work on achieving them, but who you are at your core—your values, your personality, your sense of humor, your body, and, above all, your identity as a daughter of the King—should be loved and cherished at all times. After all, God made you in *his* image. He gave you what you have and made you who you are for a reason. So embrace it all—the good, the not-so-good, and the weird. Yes, I'm saying to love the quirky parts about yourself too. Love every part of your life that makes you who you are, from opposable thumbs to dimples. Anything that makes you who you are is worth celebrating.

As I mentioned in previous chapters, we are taught to treat our bodies as temples. Don't throw away something that was given to you. Treat every part of you with the upmost care and love.

There have been many times in my life where I have faltered in loving myself. In those moments, I look at myself in the mirror and not like what I see reflecting back. I can only see the flaws and what I wish was there. In those moments, I have to remind myself that God made me exactly who he wants me to be. I have to celebrate the life he gave me. I have to be joyful. I have to look at the person in the mirror and, no matter how hard the day is, say, "You're beautiful!"

This may seem like a lot of complimenting yourself, but so what. Try it. Stand in front of the mirror and point out a few things about yourself that you feel good about. Say aloud, "I am beautiful and smart and capable!"

And in the same way you practice positive self-talk, share the love and compliment your friends. Don't be shy about pointing out your friends' amazing accomplishments. Give a compliment as simple as mentioning a great pair of earrings. You never know what's going on in someone else's life, and that one compliment may make their day and nudge them toward seeing things in a better way.

I often get a little nervous or shy when accepting a compliment because it's so nice of someone to say. People sometimes forget how much a few kind words can mean. I thank them for sharing words of love. Don't deny someone's compliment or brush it off. Instead, be thankful for the kindness someone is sharing with you and let them know you appreciate the feel-good their comment gave. It's important for you to acknowledge and receive the love you are getting and not push it away.

Challenge: Let's complement each other more often and build each other up instead of being competitive. Each day, challenge yourself to give at least one compliment to yourself and to one other person. After a week or two, bump it up to two, or maybe even three compliments each day. You may even decide to go a step further and do something kind for others each day. I think we can get better at spreading the love to one another. Keep at it and see the change that happens around you.

PRAY AND STAND STRONG

Take some time each day to sit quietly with God and check in. Talk to him about what you're excited about and what you would gently like to improve. Prayer is the best way to start your day, so my mornings usually consist of a time to reflect on myself, where I'm at, what I've accomplished, and what my next steps will be. I will take a drive, grab some hot tea on the way, and find a secluded place to just reflect and think. Sometimes I bring a journal with me to write in. It's extremely therapeutic, and helps me get a lot my feelings and thoughts out.

FACING CHALLENGES

Not to sound alarming, but there is more going on in the lives of teen girls today than ever before! When I was in high school, I was doing so many activities: going to church and youth group every week, plus making videos for my YouTube channel, and making the huge life decision not to take the traditional route to college and instead to pursue my lifelong dream of making music. And this was all happening while I was staying on top of social media, texting with my friends, figuring out my love life, keeping up with my faith, and spending time with my family.

RECONNECT WITH GOD

1. **Pray.** I know I said this only a few pages ago, but it is so important! Be consistent in prayer. Pray anytime. Find a quiet place to reconnect and start a conversation with the Lord. It doesn't have to be fancy or well-thought-out. He knows what you're trying to say. Pray to him about anything on your mind. A prayer journal is easy for me because I enjoy writing

out anything I was thinking about. You can talk to God just like you're having an open conversation too. He's listening. If you're in the car by yourself, just speak to him out loud and tell him what's been going on.

2. **Start a Bible study.** The only way to know God is to spend time with God. Ask if your youth group has small group studies. If they don't, start one. Typically, small groups meet at someone's house one night a week, where you work through a guided topical Bible study with a possible video series—often with some fun thrown in. Most studies are six to eight weeks long and are the best way to dive into the deeper understanding of the Bible. Don't be scared; you don't have to be an expert to do one. Authors like Angela Thomas and Angie Smith will gently guide you through a series, even if you don't know a thing. My senior year of high school, there was a group of five girls who met at my house every Wednesday for a Bible study. It was such a nice way to break up the week and take time to come together in fellowship.

3. **Be grateful.** Think about all God has given you and bestowed on you, and be grateful. Make a list of the people and blessings in your life that you are most grateful for. Make a list of the challenges and setbacks too. Consider what those have taught you and how they've made you stronger. When I was younger, my mom would tell me to write five things each night that I was grateful for. I would write them down in the little notebook that was on my nightstand. These types of lists can show you how much you have and how fortunate you are. It can be little and it can be simple. For instance, I'm so thankful I got another day of life!

4. **Get involved with your church.** Seek out ways to be involved. Most churches help the community by feeding the homeless, collecting used clothing or backpacks for underprivileged kids, hosting a carnival day at a local shelter, or building homes through other non-profit organizations. This is a great way to connect with like-minded people in your area—and as a bonus, you can even rack up some community service hours you may need for school. There is one mission trip that my church takes to the Union Rescue Mission (URM) center, and we put on events when we go. We've done carnival days, water fest days, and even movie nights. While we're there we talk to the people living at the URM center, and get to pour into them just like we've been poured into.

5. **Get a spiritual mentor.** Find someone—such as a pastor, a parent, or a leader at youth group—who can really pour into you spiritually. I have a mentor in her mid-twenties who encourages me in my walk with God. She speaks truth into me and helps me understand Scripture. I come to her with prayer requests and any struggles I could use encouragement with. A mentor should be older than you and typically the same gender. They should have a deeper knowledge of the Bible than you do so that they can guide and direct you.

6. **Find friends and role models of faith who encourage you.** Maybe even look to social media personalities who share your faith. Sadie Robertson, Bailee Madison, and my mom are all women who set an exemplary example of living their lives for Christ. Let their bold lives be a reminder and an encouragement to you.

It's a busy, crazy world, and there's a lot being thrown at us all of the time.

The best way to handle all of this is to seek wise advice; mine comes from the Bible and my family. It's important to me to stand by my decisions and be confident in the choices that I'm making. But even with the best intentions, the best preparation, and a little luck, it may not work out how you hoped. How you respond to challenges is even more important than how you respond to success. It ultimately impacts other choices that you make and what opportunities and roads open up for you. If you can handle yourself in tough times, you'll feel confident and poised for anything.

Handling criticism or mistakes with grace and appreciation is very difficult to do. It helps me not to lose sight of the big picture. For example, if I do poorly on a pop quiz in class, and I only

TIP Trusting your conscience is important for making good decisions, but it's a process. Do you ever hear that whisper in your mind, telling you what you know is right? Start by asking yourself the question at hand, and listen carefully to the first thought that enters your head. Once you have that decision in mind, really think about it. Your body will respond to the decision—either a lightness and relief, or a pit in your stomach. Do all of this in a quiet space with no outside distractions so you can tune in to your physical reactions, seeking God's guidance with a prayerful heart.

think about that one quiz, it can make me angry that I didn't know it was coming and I wasn't up to speed on the material. But if I think of the big picture and how my bad grade inspires me to work harder and study for the final exam, which will earn me a good grade in the class, then maybe I can appreciate the lesson it taught me. In other words, when I don't get the result I want, I can go one of two ways: I can dwell on the negativity I feel, or I can get inspired to work harder toward my goals. I think we all know which is the better option—the one that will push you toward achieving greatness!

LIVE A GOOD LIFE

There's a lot going on in the world and in *your* world as you balance school, family, friends, fun, and faith with your dreams and goals for the future. I think prioritizing is super important, and being able to make time for the things you love is what will help you live a full and well-rounded life. If you are crazed with work or school and stressing out, you should still carve out time to do an activity that makes you feel good, like painting a picture, going out for dinner with friends, or going on a hike. The truth is, doing it all is crazy hard. But that's the fun of life, don't you think? If you prioritize and put your best effort forward, you'll handle it all and enjoy the ride!

Living a good life means living according to your values and your faith. I strive to live a Christ-centered life each and every day, and I try not to compare my standard of good to the world's standard of good. I compare it to what the Lord asks of me. I try to honor my mother and father and listen to what the Lord tells me through his word.

TEN RULES TO LIVE BY

1. **Life is not fair.** Once you stop expecting everything to be fair, you can focus on what you can do for yourself. Set your goals, be prepared for opportunities, and be yourself.

2. **Be prepared to work.** Whether it's around the house to earn your allowance, at a local ice cream shop to save up for college, or keeping up with your schoolwork, you need to work hard to accomplish your goals in life. Once you embrace hard work instead of fighting it, you'll be prepared to take on your responsibilities, and you'll be that much closer to achieving your goals.

3. **No one is to blame.** You are in control of what you do. You can't blame your choices on other people's actions or words. There have been times that I've gotten into trouble, and blamed others around me because I don't want to deal with the consequences. Once you stop pointing fingers and try to make the best of your situation with a positive attitude, you'll begin to have more fun and go farther in life. You'll be able to focus on overcoming, rather than being overwhelmed.

4. **Be kind.** That's right. Be nice to everyone, from nerds to cool kids, from the principal to the janitors. Everyone is living their own lives, with their own sets of circumstances and challenges. It's not your job to judge. And it's a lot more enjoyable to be positive and friendly than to be negative and judgmental.

5. **Choose friends wisely.** Who you surround yourself with is very important to how you develop as a person. Choose posi-

tive friends who want to be there for you, build you up, and help you at the crazy turns of life. Lose the toxic friends, who don't have your best interests at heart.

6. **Be grateful.** Life is tough, but there are a lot of people who have it much worse than you. Focus on the good. Be thankful for the blessings you have, whether it's a loving family, a roof over your head, intelligence, or sense of humor. The more you celebrate the positive things, the more successful you will be.

7. **Ask for help.** Don't hesitate to reach out to trusted adults when you're feeling overwhelmed or uncertain. From your parents to a trusted family friend, a teacher, or your priest or pastor—there are a lot of adults who are looking out for you, so let them help.

8. **Plan for the future.** It's so important to set goals and dream big. You can do anything you want to in your life if you work hard and plan for success. Believe in yourself.

9. **Be happy.** To a large extent, happiness is a choice. You choose how you react to difficult situations and setbacks. You wake up every day with the power to smile, embrace your life, and spread joy. When you're older and living on your own, you'll appreciate being happy in your teen years—a time when Mom and Dad paid the bills, cooked and cleaned, and helped you.

10. **Be real.** Be the best version of you that you can be! Don't hold back. Push limits and use your gifts and talents to your advantage. Don't pretend to be anyone else but yourself.

BETTER FAITH, BETTER LIFE

My faith and my relationship with God has helped shape me in so many ways, and I know that's true for so many others. Strong beliefs inspire us to help those in need, encourage positive, optimistic attitudes, accept others' differences, and embrace true happiness. Faith has taught me so much about how to live my life. I want to be a *light* in a dark world. I want to be set apart from everyone else. I want to be different. I want to treat everyone as I want to be treated. I want to love others, as God loves me. My attitude has changed so much since God became deeply rooted in my life. I want people to see Jesus in me. I want people to look at me and say, "I wonder what she's got!"

Whatever your beliefs, you can act in a way that inspires the people around you to be better. Be kind and patient with everyone. It may sound easy, but patience can be difficult in our fast-paced world. Handle setbacks and criticism with grace, and appreciate the chance to improve. Help someone, even if it's with something easy or simple. Imagine if we all did something small but meaningful for someone else. Contributing to society with a positive act is a significant step toward a better world.

When I want to learn more about who I want to be and the kind of world I want to create, I turn to my community at church. I love my church—plain and simple. It is like one big family, who takes care of one another, supports each other, and who loves each other, even if we all don't really know each other that well. You walk in and you just feel so much love. At my church, everyone is different—from our backgrounds, races, careers, interests ... every way. When there are people of all different lifestyles in one room together worshiping the Lord, what could be greater? You can feel

LIVE HIS LIGHT DAILY

Our faith teaches us so much, but its greatest lesson is how to accept the Lord into your heart and live his light on a daily basis:

Be a good role model. No matter what you do, you're influencing younger kids around you. From siblings to younger cousins or neighbors, they're looking up to you as a role model, whether you realize it or not. So continue to make good decisions, say no to temptations, and live a good life, and maybe they will too! It's important to be that role model for your siblings. Mine look up to me, and I need to make sure I'm setting an example that they can follow.

Be positive. Did you ever hear the old saying, "If you don't have anything nice to say, don't say anything at all"? It's actually harder to do than you might think, but the idea of not contributing more negativity is enticing to me. Don't gossip. Avoid complaining. Focus on the good, and your life will seem a little more positive.

Forgive and ask for forgiveness. Anger, hostility, and resentment all breed more anger, hostility, and resentment, so let it go. When someone does something to offend you and honestly apologizes, accept it and move on. And when you've made a mistake, own it and apologize immediately.

Love fiercely. Embrace your family and friends and support them. And love the Lord, just like he loves you. Strive to live each day with this love in your heart, letting it guide you as you treat others kindly and lovingly.

> **Pray daily.** Do you want to know the best way to accomplish all of the above? Pray. Notice that I say this again? I can't express how important this really is. Take the time to sit quietly, reflect, and pray each and every day. You'll feel centered, connected, and motivated to live it to the fullest.

the unifying energy of our shared love for Jesus swirling around the room. I can't express to you how happy it makes me. When I'm at church, I am either in tears of joy or I have a gigantic smile on my face because I can't contain my happiness.

I'd like to take that energy, that passion, and that desire to make the world a better place and amplify it. I know that by acting according to my faith and bringing light into the world, I'm making it just a little better. I wish we could all do that!

LOVE AS GOD LOVES YOU

You'll hear so many people telling you to "love yourself" and "be selfish and self-care." While loving yourself and taking care of yourself is important, and doing so serves as the basis for good self-esteem, loving those around you is even more important. Giving back to the community not only helps other people, it makes you feel amazing too. I honestly can say there is nothing quite like the feeling of serving others with an open heart.

A lot of people, no matter whether they're teens or adults, go through times when they feel there's something missing in life. Like there's a hole that needs to be filled, or a purpose they haven't found. This is true for a lot of Christians too. God made us as a community. He created us to be his hands and feet—to care for each other. He created us to fill that emptiness within one another. When you serve those around you, you are filling a need for them, and God is filling you with love and compassion.

Every Christmas morning for the past couple of years, my family and I have gone to a homeless shelter and cooked breakfast for the families who live there. We make food, eat, and sing Christmas carols together. It's a blast and the best way to start my Christmas day. It helps us all focus on what's truly important—not the gifts under the tree, not the amazing food waiting for dinner, not even our favorite holiday movies, but serving others. Spending Christmas morning at the homeless shelter really warms my heart and shows me how much I have to be grateful for. I am so fortunate in this life to have the things that I do; giving back to the community reminds me of this, and that we need to do what we can to reach out in our world.

Take a look around you, at the people both within and outside of your community. Is there anything you do that connects you and lifts others up? Or have you never thought too much about it? It's never the wrong time to step outside of yourself and be more than you are. Look for opportunities big and small in your area to start getting involved and building a better community. Start with your school or church and see what programs they might offer. Or try websites like dosomething.org, which list tons of volunteer opportunities all over the country. You may enjoy it so much that you want to take on a bigger trip that includes a dedicated week, month, or even a year of service.

Do something, no matter how small. Even if it's as simple as shoveling the snow from your neighbor's walkway, or taking the trash to the curb if you know they struggle with it.

SO MANY WAYS TO GET INVOLVED!

When you decide to become involved in your community, whether locally or around the world, it can be tough to get started. You may not know where to start, or who to connect with. But there are tons of ways to get information and find something you can really do well.

- Talk to your church or youth group leader
- Look into local hospital or food bank opportunities
- Talk to your high school or college counselor, or administration office
- Search nationwide sites, such as: Skip1.org, Compassion.com, Children's Hunger Fund, WorldVision.org, Starlight Foundation, lollipoptheater.org, Peach's Neet Feet, kindcampaign.com. Another site I love is urm.org.
- Search the Internet using keywords like *youth community service* and *youth mission trips*
- Look into world mission sites like Teen Missions International or Campus Crusade for Christ
- Call your local Christian television or radio station for opportunities and recommendations
- Offer your faith story if the opportunity arises, but know that just being there to serve is an act of witnessing

DREAM BIG!

Never be afraid to dream big! *The Voice* gave me the most incredible opportunity to share what I'm passionate about with millions of people! I was able to improve so much from the feedback and support I got from my coach, and from the high-pressure atmosphere. For that, I am so grateful. Auditioning for *The Voice* is a big dream in and of itself, and if that's what you want, then go for it. Don't be afraid to fail or make a mistake. Do everything in your power to achieve your dreams, no matter how big!

You may not know everything you need to know—and maybe you never will know it all! But you should be able to listen to your gut and know the difference between the right and wrong path. Follow your conscience and that little voice in your head that tells you what you should and shouldn't do. Remember

TIP How to stay safe when serving others

Serving the community can be extremely rewarding, and a way to give of yourself freely. But it's very important to stay safe and away from dangerous situations. Here are some tips for staying safe:

- Get a group together to serve
- Do everything in pairs
- Go with a church group
- Check out the organization and ask around in order to make sure it's reputable and keeps volunteers safe
- Be aware of your surroundings
- Try to know what you're doing/volunteering for before you go
- Make sure you ask about any training you may need before you start

that the choices you make reflect who you are and what you stand for. They are no one else's choices but yours.

BE PATIENT WITH YOURSELF

Remember, change takes time. You don't become the person you want to be overnight, so be patient and consistent. Enjoy the journey. You might not finish this book with total clarity on the real, authentic you and how you want to live. But it's a start.

Patience is one of the most important qualities you can have. Impatience and making decisions impulsively tends to lead to very mixed results, and often unpleasant ones. I'm particularly impatient anytime I'm learning something new. I don't want to sit through hours of lectures and practice. I just want to know it all at once. When I first started playing the piano, I would get so frustrated during my lessons because I just wanted to be a pro already. Unfortunately, it doesn't work that way. Even now, I have needed to stick with certain things that I'm learning, and accept the fact that things take time. Taking time to understand, to learn, and to figure things out is what life is about. Patience is key, and keeping that in mind will help you so much.

I hope that by sharing my experiences, missteps, successes, and the tips I've learned the hard way, you feel like you're not alone in whatever struggles you're dealing with. And because we're all dealing with many of the same crazy issues, I also hope you can reach out to a friend and talk about your problems openly. I want to break down the walls we put up to make us seem perfectly together to everyone else. We're all humans living in a hectic world, and perfection is impossible. Let's open up and share the hard things we're working through, whether it's boy issues or gossip, mental health or a bad breakout. If we combine our experiences and wisdom, we could rule the world!

You have the power to live the life you want, and one of the most important ways to do that is to pave your own path. Don't be afraid to go outside of the box. Don't be afraid to push the limits and to see what you're capable of. If you have a dream, go for it! Don't worry about what others around you are doing—or not doing. Focus on yourself, your goals, and your journey. You can achieve anything you put your mind to.